ETHICS
and the
FUTURE
of
CAPITALISM

THE LEARNED SOCIETY OF PRAXIOLOGY

PRAXIOLOGY:
The International Annual of Practical Philosophy and Methodology
Vol. 9

EDITOR-IN-CHIEF
Wojciech W. Gasparski
The Institute of Philosophy and Sociology
Polish Academy of Sciences
Nowy Świat Str. 72, 00-330 Warsaw, Poland

ETHICS
and the
FUTURE
of
CAPITALISM

Praxiology:
The International Annual of
Practical Philosophy and
Methodology

Volume 9

edited by
László Zsolnai
in cooperation with
Wojciech W. Gasparski

Transaction Publishers
New Brunswick (U.S.A.) and London (U.K.)

Copyright © 2002 by Transaction Publishers, New Brunswick, New Jersey, U.S.A.

Preparation of this volume was partly financed by Komitet Badán Naukowych (The Committee for Scientific Research)

This book is printed on acid-free paper that meets the American National Standard for Permanence of Paper for Printed Library Materials.

Library of Congress Catalog Number: 2001052298
ISBN: 0-7658-0120-5
Printed in the United States of America

Library of Congress Cataloging-in-Publication Data

Ethics and the future of capitalism / edited by László Zsolnai in cooperation with Wojciech W. Gasparski.
    p. cm.—(Praxiology: v. 9)
    Against market fundamentalism : "The capitalist threat" reconsidered / George Soros with Andrew Brody...[et al.]—Ethics of capitalism / Peter Koslowski—Misunderstood and abused liberalism / Lubomír Mlčoch—Humanizing the economy : on the relationship between the ethics of human rights and economic discourse / Stefano Zamagni—The possibility of stakeholder capitalism / R. Edward Freeman—Effectiveness, efficiencey, and ethicality in business and management / Wojciech W. Gasparski—Responsibility and management / László Zsolnai.
    Includes bibliographical references.
    ISBN 0-7658-0120-5 (cloth : alk. paper)
    1. Capitalism—Moral and ethical aspects. 2. Economics—Moral and ethical aspects. 3. International trade—Moral and ethical aspects. 4. Globalization—Moral and ethical aspects. 5. Business ethics. 6. Human rights. 7. Capitalism—Moral and ethical aspects—Europe, Eastern. I. Zsolnai, László. II. Gasparski, Wojciech. III. Praxiology (New Brunswick, N.J.) ; v. 9.

HB501 .E77695 2002
330.12'2—dc21
                                            2001052298

Contents

Editorial

Wojciech W. Gasparski
Institute of Philosophy and Sociology
Polish Academy of Sciences
Warsaw, Poland

There is a dispute lasting over a century between those who believe that capitalism is immoral in itself and those who advocate it as a system establishing just behavior by itself. It is R. Edward Freeman who writes: "The rise of capitalism in the West, the Industrial Revolution, and the emergence of socialism and Marxism fundamentally changed the relationship between business and ethics.[1] The Marxist critique of the industrial world of the nineteenth century raised questions about the moral nature of the dominant business system. The labor movement made these questions real, as owners and workers often resorted to violence to settle their differences." (Freeman 1991, 4). It was Ludwig von Mises, an Austrian[2] praxiologist and economist who – being afraid that the belief of capitalism reformers that it would be possible to "dethrone the Moloch of capitalism without enthroning the Moloch state" (p. 724) – wrote the following:

> The arbitrary value judgments which are at the bottom of these opinions need not concern us here. What these critics blame capitalism for is irrelevant; their errors and fallacies are beside the point. [...]
> In the market economy the individual is free to act within the orbit of private property and the market. His choices are final. For his fellow men his actions are data which they must take into account in their own acting. The coordination of the autonomous action of all individuals is accomplished by the operation of the

market. Society does not tell a man what to do and what not to do. There is no need to enforce cooperation by special orders or prohibitions. Noncooperation penalizes itself. Adjustment to the requirements of society's productive effort and the pursuit of the individual's own concerns are not in conflict. Consequently no agency is required to settle such conflicts. The system can work and accomplish its tasks without the interference of an authority issuing special orders and prohibitions and punishing those who do not comply. (Mises 1966, 724–725).

Mises considered reformers plans "that along with norms designed for the protection and preservation of private property further ethical rules should be ordained " (p. 725) erroneous. It was, and still is – see, e.g., (Barry 2000) – the point of view characteristic for an ideal model of capitalism with perfect competition in the market assuring equilibrium. The difference between «ideal» and «real» markets, however, is of such a nature that real markets need ethical dimension to be moral [Boatright 1999; Mackenzie and Lewis 1999]. Praxiology, being necessary, is not enough. This is why the *Human Action in Business* (Vol. 5 of the *Praxiology: The International Annual of Practical Philosophy and Methodology* series) was equipped with a subtitle *Praxiological and Ethical Dimensions*. Norman Bowie, one of its contributors, stated in his article the following:

> Most discussion of business ethics focuses on ethics as a contrast on profit. On this view ethics and profit are inversely related; the more ethical a business is the less profitable it is, the more profitable the business is the less ethical it will be. While I admit that there are times when doing the morally correct thing will reduce profits, I reject the common characterization of an inverse relationship between ethics and profits. In this lecture I argue that there is frequently a positive relation between ethics and profits; normally ethics enhances the bottom line rather than diminishing it. Indeed I will argue the stronger thesis that in a world where many doubt the existence a positive relation between ethics and profits, ethics can be a source of competitive advantage. The ethical firm will have an above average profit, other things being equal. (Bowie 1996, 365).

Later on, in another paper, Bowie added that "if the adoption of a Kantian theory of capitalist firms could provide a universal morality for business, provide meaningful work for employees, institute firms as moral communities and help establish a more cosmopolitan and peaceful world – as Bowie believes it can do – Kantian capitalism will have done everything any theory of business ethics could do. There may be other ways to achieve this end, but the Kantian theory of capitalism offers one clear blueprint." (Bowie 1998, 56–57) Other attempts to achieve the end are formulated in this book, therefore the book should be considered as a companion volume to the previous ones in the series: the mentioned *Human Action in Business: Praxiological and Ethical Dimensions* (Vol. 5) and the *Business Students Focus on Ethics* (Vol. 8).

Paraphrasing the title of the article by Linda K. Trevino and Gary R. Weaver (Trevino and Weaver 1994) one may ask a question: is this book about ETICS of capitalism or about ethics of CAPITALISM? The answer is similar to the two-part thesis of Joseph Betz:

> First, business ethics exists quite apart from politics in matter of simple, basic ethical norms like those prohibiting lying, wanton injury, and sexual harassment [...] Second, there are issues in business ethics which do not represent a settled and shared common ethics. They represent a choice between competing, almost equally attractive, values. These problems in business ethics can only have a political solution. Politics here represents the commitment to basic values and will represent liberal and conservative extremes or some compromise in between. The solution accepted for these problems will change with the political climate and era and will be unstable. We should strive to keep the basic, simple settled ethical issues in business out of politics, and we should strive to be frank about our political differences as we needfully politicize the solutions to the more complex, unsettled problems in business ethics. (Betz 1998)

Thus, it is ETHICS of CAPITALISM, where "ethics" stands for responsibility and duty while "capitalism" stands for both: (i) the way to solve value dependent problems needing political solutions[3], (ii) an engineering – mainly financial – of exchange, based nowadays gradually on knowledge (Drucker 1993). Capitalism needs ethics for nothing should serve its own judge; ethics role is to monitor, audit and assess solutions and behavior of actors playing games on the capitalistic stage. Ethics role is also to formulate – on the basis of its inquiry – standards defining the bottom line for further activities.

Ethics is one of the important component of the open society, the idea raised by Karl R. Popper and intensely promoted by George Soros, an effective capital investor and a philanthropist. Ironically enough it is he who is afraid that the very idea is endangered nowadays. By what? By crisis of global capitalism, as the title of his recent book reads.

> Money has certain attributes that intrinsic values lack: It has a common denominator, it can be quantified, and it is appreciated by practically everyone. These are the attributes that qualify money as a medium of exchange, but no necessarily as the ultimate goal. Most of the benefits attached to money accrue from spending it; in this respect money serve as a means to an end. Only in one respect does money serve as the ultimate goal: when the goal is to accumulate wealth.

Far be it from me to belittle the benefits of wealth; but to make the accumulation of wealth the ultimate goal disregards many other aspects of existence that also deserve consideration, particularly from those who have satisfied their material needs for survival. I cannot specify what those other aspects of existence are; it is in the nature of intrinsic values that they cannot be reduced to a common denominator and they are not equally appreciated by everyone. Thinking people are entitled to decide for themselves-it is a privilege they enjoy once they have met the requirements of survival. But instead of enjoying the privilege, we have gone out of our way to abdicate from it by giving such prominence to the accumulation of wealth. When everybody is striving for more money, competition becomes so intense that even the most successful are reduced to the position of having to fight for survival. [...] The autonomy and discretion enjoyed by the privileged in the past has been lost. I believe we are poorer for it. There ought to be more to life than survival. But the survival of the fittest has become the goal of our civilization.

Does the concept of open society imply a different set of values? I believe it does but I must be careful how I present the case. Open society certainly requires the correction of errors and excesses but it also recognizes the absence of an objective criterion by which they can be judged. I can argue that the promotion of the profit motive into an ethical principle is an aberration but I cannot set myself up as the ultimate arbiter who adjudicates in the name of open society. What I can say with confidence is that the substitution of monetary values for all other values is pushing society toward a dangerous disequilibrium and suppressing human aspirations that deserve to be considered as seriously as the growth of GNP. (Soros 1998, pp. 207–208).

Soros arguments are simple and speak for themselves:

Profit maximizing behavior follows the dictates of expediency and ignores the demands of morality. Financial markets are not immoral; they are amoral. By contrast, collective decision making cannot function properly without drawing a distinction between right and wrong. We do not *know* what is right. If we did, we would not need a democratic government; we could live happily under the rule of a philosopher king as Plato proposed. But we must have a sense of what is right and what is wrong, an inner light that guides our behavior as citizens and politicians. Without it, representative democracy cannot work. The profit motive dims the inner light. [...]

There is also another argument to be considered. Whether people will be satisfied with an open society will depend a great deal on the results that an open society can produce. The strongest argument in favor of open society is that it offers infinite scope for improvement. Being reflexive, open society needs to be reinforced by the results. The results in turn depend on what is considered satisfactory. Progress is a subjective idea, as much dependent on people's values as on material conditions of life. [...] Intrinsic values cannot be measured in monetary terms. We need some other measure of happiness, even if it cannot be quantified. In my opinion, the autonomy that citizens enjoy would be a better measure, because there ought to be more to life than survival. (Soros 1998, pp. 208–209).

This book consisting of papers devoted to the topic of ethical dimension of capitalism is a collective contribution to the debate of the future development of the system of economic life in a globalized world in which capitalism dominates and its relations with the society and individuals the society – hopefully open – is composed of. This is not just a topic of another academic debate only. Quite the contrary. It is a real problem – one may even say a hot topic – of contemporary societies of different cultures, of different levels of the development, of different weltanschaung, different fears, hopes and beliefs trying to formulate the problem in an adequate way in order to solve it not only effectively and efficiently but also according to the moral norms of ethics.

* * *

It is with great sorrow to let the readers know that Professor Tadeusz Pszczołowski, a member of the International Advisory Board of this Annual died on 17 December 1999 at the age of seventy-seven. Prof. Pszczołowski, a student of Tadeusz Kotarbiński, the founder of Polish praxiology, was a former Head of Praxiology Department at the Polish Academy of Sciences. He published several books and numerous papers on praxiology and theory of organization. Pszczołowski served for many years as the editor-in-chief of a Polish periodical *Prakseologia* and later of a Polish quarterly *Zagadnienia naukoznawstwa* (Science Studies).

He and I edited a book *Praxiological Studies: Polish Contributions to the Science of Efficient Action*, Reidel – PWN, 1983 which made the Polish praxiology known outside Poland. It was Mario Bunge who acknowledged it in his *Treatise on Basic Philosophy*. The book *Praxiological Studies* may be considered an ancestor in a way of *Praxiology: The International Annual of Practical Philosophy and Methodology*.

References

Barry, N., 2000, *Business Ethics*, Purdue University Press, West Lafayette, Indiana.

Berger, P. L., 1994, *The Capitalist Spirit: Toward a Religious Ethic of Wealth Creation*, Polish translation, Znak Publishers, Cracow (original publ. ISC Press, San Francisco, CA).

Betz, J., 1998, Business Ethics and Politics, *Business Ethics Quarterly*, Vol. 8:4, pp. 693–702.

Boatright, J. R., 1999, *Presidential Address: Does Business Ethics Rest on a Mistake?*, *Business Ethics Quarterly*, Vol. 9:4, pp. 583–591.

Bowie, N. E., 1996, The Moral Foundation of Capitalism, in: W. W. Gasparski and L. V. Ryan, eds., *Human Action in Business: Praxiological and Ethical Dimensions*, Transaction, New Brunswick (USA)–London (UK), pp. 365–382.

Bowie, N. E., 1998, A Kantian Theory of Capitalism, *Business Ethics Quarterly*, Special Issue No. 1, pp. 37–60.

Drucker, P. F., 1993, *Post-capitalist Society*, Butterworth-Heinemann, Oxford.

Epstein, E. M., 2000, The Continuing Quest for Accountable, Ethical, and Human Corporate Capitalism: An Enduring Challenge for Social Issues in Management in the New Millennium, *Business Ethics Quarterly*, Vol. 10:1, pp. 145–157.

Freeman, R. E., ed., 1991, *Business Ethics: The State of the Art*, Oxford University Press, New York.

Freeman, R. E. and Phillips, R. A., 1996, Efficiency, Effectiveness and Ethics: A Stakeholder View, in: W. W. Gasparski and L. V. Ryan, eds., *Human Action in Business: Praxiological and Ethical Dimensions*, Transaction, New Brunswick (USA)–London (UK), pp. 65–81.

Mackenzie, C. and Lewis, A., 1999, Morals and Markets: The Case of Ethical Investing, *Business Ethics Quarterly*, Vol. 9:3, pp. 439–452.

Selznick, P., 1992, *The Moral Commonwealth: Social Theory and the Promise of Community*, Berkeley and Los Angeles, The University of California Press.

Soros, G., 1998, *The Crisis of Global Capitalism [Open Society Endangered]*, Little, Brown and Company, London.

Trevino, L. K. and Weaver, G. R., 1994, Business ETHICS/BUSINESS Ethics: One Field or Two?, *Business Ethics Quarterly*, Vol. 4:2, pp. 113–128.

Notes

1. For a definitive account see Fernand Braudel, *The Structure of Everyday Life* (New York: Harper & Row, 1981). For a different point of view see Nathan Rosenberg and L. E. Birdzell, Jr., *How the West Grew Rich* (New York: Basic Books, 1986).
2. Since late nineteen forties he has developing his studies in the United States.
3. "It is interesting to note that during the first decade of the SIM [Social Issues in Management] Division [of the Academy of Management], 'Ethics' per se was not a dominant area of interest [...]. Not until the 1980s did we begin in a major way to focus our attention through the lens of ethical analysis on the behavior of individual businesspersons, the policies, processes, and practices of business organizations and the macro character and implications of corporate culture and conduct. [...] As an area of inquiry business ethics and, more broadly, the values underlying our business culture pose the real 'bottom line' issues for what Philip Selznick has termed a Moral Commonwealth [Selznick 1992], irrespective of their state of trendiness (or lack of the same) in popular and business circles at a given moment in time." [Epstein 2000, 149–150].

Preface

László Zsolnai
Business Ethics Center
Budapest University of Economic Sciences
Hungary

In the Millennium capitalism is at a crossroad. By the *collapse* of *communism* and the accelerated trend of *globalization* certainly a new stage of capitalism has arrived. Protest actions that happened in 1999 and 2000 in Seattle and Washington as well as in Millau and Prague clearly show that the *legitimacy of capitalism* is questionable in many respects. Sociological surveys in Eastern and Central Europe shows that a considerable part of the population is unable to accept capitalism as an economic system.

The moral foundation of capitalism should be re-considered and re-newed. This was the main function of the *Ethics of Capitalism* summer course that was held at the Central European University (CEU) in July 6–17, 1998 in Budapest.

In the CEU summer course 28 young scholars participated from 12 countries. Lecturers included Edward R. Freeman (Darden Business School, University of Virginia, USA), Lubomír Mlčoch (Charles University, Prague, Czech Republic), Wojciech W. Gasparski (Polish Academy of Sciences, Warsaw, Poland), Peter Koslowski (Hannover Institute for Philosophy, Germany), Stefano Zamagni (University of Bologna, Italy) and László Zsolnai (Budapest University of Economic Sciences, Hungary). We got invaluable help from Eva Gedeon, the

Director of the Central European University Summer Program for organizing our course.

As a pre-program event to the CEU SUN course, on June 22, 1998 we organized a public debate with George Soros on his influential paper "The Capitalist Threat" that was published in the Atlantic Monthly in 1997 February. Discussants included Andrew Brody (Institute of Economics, Hungarian Academy of Sciences), Olivier Giscard d'Estaing (INSEAD & Business Association of World Social Summit, Paris), Ferenc Rabár (Budapest University of Economic Sciences) and Jörn Rüsen (Kulturwissenschaftliches Institut, Essen). For organizing the public debate we got important support from Istvan Teplan, Executive Vice-President of the Central European University and Andras Nemeslaki, former Academic Director of IMC – Graduate School of Business.

The present book is based on the lectures and discussions of the CEU summer course and the Soros debate; however, in the last two years contributors had the opportunity to develop their arguments further. We received helpful comments from Edwin M. Epstein (St. Mary's College of California & UC Berkeley) and Henri-Claude de Bettignies (INSEAD and Stanford University) on an earlier version of the manuscript.

The book is organized in seven chapters. The first chapter is the paper *Against Market Fundamentalism: "The Capitalist Threat" Reconsidered* which is the edited and extended version of the Soros debate. Here George Soros has introduced his new term "market fundamentalism" referring to a view according to which all kind of human values can be reduced to market values. Andrew Brody, Olivier Giscard d'Estaing, Ferenc Rabár, and Jörn Rüsen carefully discussed and developed further Soros' main argument that *laissez-faire capitalism* undermines the very values on which *open* and *democratic societies* depend.

Soros' final words in the debate can get strong recognition: the instabilities and inequalities of the capitalist system could feed into nationalistic, ethnic and religious fundamentalism. It is exactly why we should prevent a return to that kind of fundamentalism by *correcting* the excesses of *market fundamentalism.*

The second chapter is Peter Koslowski's paper *Ethics of Capitalism.* Koslowski's main thesis is that *capitalism* constitutes a necessary component of a *free society* but considering capitalist economic order as to be the whole society falls short of social reality. He strongly emphasizes that capitalist economy can show the individuals the *relative prices* and the *optimal allocation* of *resources* but cannot relieve them of the choice between goals and values. For exactly this reason there is a need for *reembedding* business, the market, and economic motivation into *ethical* and *social norms*. Capitalism should be reembedded in the ethics and culture of a society.

The third chapter is Lubomír Mlčoch's paper *Misunderstood and Abused Liberalism*. The paper focuses on the *problematic* of *Czech style capitalism*. Mlčoch argues that introducing *laissez-faire capitalism* without respecting the *cultural norms and institutional settings* of a society necessarily leads to great *inefficiency* and enormous *social losses*.

The fourth chapter is Stefano Zamagni's paper *Humanizing the Economy: On the Relationship Between Ethics of Human Rights and Economic Discourse* in which he investigates the role of *civil society* in relation to the market and the state. Zamagni shows that civil society is based on *reciprocity* whose role is vital in the functioning of advanced market economies. Reciprocity ties may modify the outcome of the economic game either by stabilizing *co-operative behavior* of the agents or by altering *endogenously* the *preferences* of the agents themselves. Zamagni believes that civil society can contribute significantly to the *development* of capitalism, which is both *sustainable* and *just*.

The fifth chapter is Edward R. Freeman's paper *The Possibility of Stakeholder Capitalism*. By the term "stakeholder" Freeman refers to those groups, which can affect and are affected by the corporation. He argues that stakeholder relationship is a key to understand the functioning of business in the today's world. Freeman defines different principles by which *stakeholder capitalism* allows the possibility that *business* becomes a *fully human institution* that asks managers to *create value* for *all stakeholders*.

The sixth chapter is a paper by Wojciech W. Gasparski entitled *Effectiveness, Efficiency, and Ethicality in Business and Management*. Gasparski introduces the *praxiology tradition* in the debate about ethical aspects of capitalism. Influenced by the thoughts of Kotarbiński and von Mises, Gasparski states a *"triple E"* criteria for judging economic actions, namely effectiveness, efficiency, and ethics. A well-functioning economy should satisfy all these criteria simultaneously. Some *religious perspective* is provided to defend the "triple E" model.

The seventh chapter is my own paper *Responsibility and Profit Making* in which the conditions of ethical and social acceptability of profit making are explored. *Responsibility* is introduced as providing criteria for *acceptable business practices*. I argue that profit is *ethically accept-*

able if it is produced by activities that in aggregate do not violate the applying ethical norms. Profit is *socially acceptable* if it is produced by activities that in aggregate do not cause harm to the stakeholders. Hence *non-violence* emerges as a necessary condition of acceptable business practices.

January 17, 2001

Introduction

László Zsolnai
Business Ethics Center
Budapest University of Economic Sciences
Hungary

The papers in this book constitute some kind of a manifesto. The authors share the conviction that the *business ethics* and the *future* of *capitalism* are strongly connected. If we want to *sustain capitalism* for a long time we certainly have to create a *less violent, more caring* form of it.

George Soros has developed a strong argument that *laissez faire capitalism* undermines the very values on which open and democratic societies depend. While national capitalism was socially constrained and politically regulated, present day *global capitalism* is basically *unconstrained* and *unregulated*. Soros calls the underlying ideology of global capitalism as *market fundamentalism*. Market fundamentalism is a belief according to which all kind of values can be reduced to *market values* and *free market* is the only efficient mechanism that can provide rational allocation of resources.

The market as an *evaluation mechanism* has its inherent deficiencies. First of all, there are *stakeholders* that are simply *non-represented* in determining market values. *Natural beings* and *future generations* do not have the opportunity to vote on the marketplace. Secondly, the preferences of *human individuals* count rather unequally, that is, in proportion to their purchasing power; the interests of the *poor* and disadvantageous *people* are necessarily *underrepresented* in free market settings. Thirdly, the actual preferences of the *market players* are rather *self--centered* and *myopic*; that is, economic agents make their own decisions regarding short-term consequences only.

These inherent deficiencies imply that free markets cannot produce socially optimal outcomes. In many cases *market evaluation* is definitely misleading from a social or environmental point of view. It means that market is a *necessary* but *not a sufficient form* of evaluating economic activities. *Alternative evaluation* of economic activities by the techniques of *environmental* and *social reporting, accounting*, and *auditing* is also needed. Since both market and alternative evaluations are *fallible* the simultaneous application of them, that is, some kind of a *triangulation* is badly needed providing a fair and accurate picture about economic activities.

Global capitalism does need counter-veiling forces. Both *international politics* and *transnational civil society* could play important roles in correcting the deficiencies of market fundamentalism. The instabilities and inequalities of the global capitalist system could feed into nationalistic, ethnic and religious fundamentalism. It is exactly why we should prevent a return to that kind of fundamentalism by *correcting* the excesses of *laissez faire capitalism* on a global scale.

Koslowski notes that three structural features can characterize *capitalism* as an *economic order*, namely *private property* of the means of production, *profit* and *utility maximization* as basic motivation for economic action, and co-ordination of economic activities by the *market* and *price mechanism*. Modern capitalism is *disembedded* from the social and cultural norms of society. The capitalist economy can show the individuals the *relative prices* and the *optimal allocation* of *resources* but cannot relieve them of the choice between goals and values.

From the perspective of *ethics* the question about goals that individuals in a society set for themselves is as important as how these goals are to be fulfilled. One must ask about the *reasonableness* of the *goals* as well as the *optimal allocation* of *resources* for those goals. *Pareto-optimum* cannot define social or ethical optimality *beyond* the economic viewpoint of *allocative optimality*. Ethics requires *considering* and *balancing* the *totality* of *aspects* and not making decisions or evaluations solely on the basis of individual preferences.

Market does not properly deal with *certain values* (public goods, cultural goods, and the environment). A society, which bases the pursuit of its goals on one normative principle only, is *not* able to realize the *good*. There is a need for *reembedding* business, the market, and economic motivation into *ethical* and *social norms*. Capitalism should be *reembedded* in the ethics and culture of *society*.

Mlčoch underlines that introducing *laissez faire capitalism* in Eastern and Central Europe without respecting the *cultural norms* and *institutional settings* of society necessarily leads to great *inefficiency* and enormous *social losses*. Transitional economies show that there is a possible *trade off* between the *speed* of institutional change and the emerging business *ethics* and *legal* and *economic order*. *Fast institutional changes* could *destabilize* society and economy, endanger order, and undermine moral standards in business.

The economy is necessarily based on *meta-economic values* that should not focus on economic efficiency only. The *Czech style capitalism*, which sacrificed ethical considerations in order to achieve economic rationalization and efficiency, was simply doomed to fail. *Business ethics* is *not* a *luxury* for advanced economies but a source of the *wealth* of *nations*.

Societies of *success* enable people to undertake co-operative ventures for mutual advantages. In such societies – Zamagni argues – the so-called *social capital* is well developed that is an efficient network of *non-profit* and *voluntary organizations* functions to provide public good of various kind. *Reciprocity* plays a vital role in the functioning of advanced market economies. Reciprocity ties may increase the outcome of the economic game either by stabilizing *co-operative behavior* of the agents or by altering *endogenously* the *preferences* of the agents themselves.

The most *detrimental effect* of the *self-interest doctrine* and the *culture* of *contract* is to believe that behaviors inspired by other motive than self-interest is conducive to economic disaster. Quite the contrary, *trust, reciprocity* and *altruism* contribute significantly to the civilization process our societies are undergoing.

The *civil society*, which is based on the *principle* of *subsidiarity* and functions by the *mechanism* of *reciprocity*, could contribute significantly to the development of capitalism, which is *environmentally sustainable* and *socially just*. The post-modern, global reality of our age requires a *new model* of social and economic *governance* that is a constructive symbiosis if the *invisible hand* of the *market*, the *visible hand* of the *government*, and the *humanizing hand* of *civil society*.

The *stakeholder relationship* is a key to understand the functioning of business in the today's world. Freeman emphasizes that identifying and analyzing stakeholders is a way to acknowledge the existence of *multiple constituencies* in a corporation. The more the stakeholders *participate* in the decisions that affect them, the greater the likelihood that they will be *committed* to the future of the corporate enterprise.

Stakeholder capitalism is determined by principles that allow the possibility that *business* becomes a *fully human institution* that asks managers to *create value* for *all stakeholders*. The *Principle of Stakeholder Co-operation* says that value is created because stakeholders can jointly satisfy their needs and desires. The *Principle of Complexity* says that human beings are complex creatures capable of acting from different values. The *Principle of Continuous Creation* says that business, as an institution is a source of the creation of value. The *Principle of Emergent Competition* says that competition emerges from a relatively free and democratic society so that stakeholders have options.

Stakeholder capitalism bases our understanding and expectations of business not on the worst that we *can do* but on the *best*. It is a way that allows seeing *business* as an institution that is a *vital part* of our conception of the *good life*.

Gasparski shows that the *praxiology* tradition provides a *"triple E"* criteria for judging economic actions, namely *effectiveness*, *efficiency*, and *ethics*. A well-functioning economy should satisfy all these criteria *simultaneously*.

In the context of contemporary global capitalism a *new form* of ethical and social *justification* of *profit making* is certainly needed. *Responsibility* plays a central role in providing criteria for acceptable business practices. Responsibility means *caring* for the *beings* involved in our actions whether they are *human* beings, *non-human* being or *future* human beings.

The *ethical performance* of an organization can be assessed by seeing its activities from the *deontological* (i.e. norm regarding) perspective. It implies that profit is *ethically acceptable* if it is produced by activities that in aggregate *do not violate* the applying ethical norms. The *social performance* of an organization can be assessed by seeing its activities from the *stakeholder* (i.e. other regarding) perspective. It implies that profit is *socially acceptable* if it is produced by activities that in aggregate *do not cause harm* to the stakeholders.

Following James Robertson, one of the most influential alternative economists of our age, I propose to accept two distinct but interrelated principles that business organizations should realize in order to be legitimate in the 21st century reality. (1) Business should be *conserving* that is, should contribute to the conservation and restoration of the ecology of the natural world. (2) Business should be *enabling*, that is, should contribute to the enhancement of the capabilities and self-development of people.

Conserving and enabling call for a *radical transformation* of *business*. The future of capitalism, I believe, highly depends on its ability to adapt to the challenges of the ecological age we live in now.

Against Market Fundamentalism: "The Capitalist Threat" Reconsidered

George Soros
with
Andrew Brody, Olivier Giscard d'Estaing,
Ferenc Rabár and Jörn Rüsen

On June 22, 1998 the Business Ethics Center of the Budapest University of Economic Sciences, the Central European University Summer Program, and the IMC Graduate School of Business organized a public debate with George Soros on his influential paper "The Capitalist Threat" published by *The Atlantic Monthly* in February 1997. Discussants included Andrew Brody (Institute of Economics, Hungarian Academy of Sciences), Olivier Giscard d'Estaing (INSEAD & Business Association for World Social Summit, Paris), Ferenc Rabár (Budapest University of Economic Sciences), and Jörn Rüsen (Kulturwissenschaftliches Institute, Essen). The discussion was focused on Soros' main argument, that *laissez faire capitalism* undermines the very values on which *open* and *democratic societies* depend.

The following paper is based on the recorded material of the debate. It was edited by György Pataki of the Business Ethics Center, Budapest University of Economic Sciences.

George Soros:

Before I start criticizing the *global capitalist system*, I should first make sure that there is such a thing as a global capitalist system. It is generally recognized that there is a global economy and it is characterized not only by the free movement of goods and services but, particularly, by the *free movement* of *capital*. That is, I believe what makes it possible to speak of a global capitalist system. Since capital moves more easily than the other factors of production, like labor and land, it will always seek, when it is free to move the place where the conditions are the most advantageous. Capital, thus, tends to avoid taxation and regulation. That makes it very difficult to tax and regulate capital and it does put capital in an advantageous position, which was not there before this global capitalist system has evolved.

The global capitalist system is actually quite a *new phenomenon*. Though we have had increasingly globalized trade since the Second World War, if you look back to that time there was absolutely no movement of capital internationally. It is difficult to say when exactly the global capitalist system came into existence because it was a gradual development. Certainly a crucial moment was around the 1980s when President Reagan was elected in the USA and Margaret Thatcher was elected in Britain. They had a certain view of how the market should be allowed to operate. Today financial markets have a tremendous influence on what happens in each particular country.

Of course, I am a supporter of the capitalist system and, when I criticize it, I am not advocating the abolishment of the capitalist system but I am arguing that it is *imperfect* and it has deficiencies and, unless the deficiencies are corrected, probably the system will become *intolerable* and *unsustainable*.

My critique basically falls into two major categories: one is the *deficiency* of the *market system* and the second is the *deficiencies* of the *non-market sector* of *society*. My criticism is better grounded as far as the market system is concerned. But I think that the deficiencies of the non-market sector, the political system, national and international politics, and social values, the lack of a global society to correspond to a global economy, are more profound and more important.

The first is a quite fundamental critique of our interpretation of how financial markets operate. The prevailing view based on *economic theory* is that financial markets tend towards equilibrium. I contend that this is actually a *false view* of *financial markets*. Equilibrium is not appropriate for understanding how financial markets operate. It is based on a false analogy with physics where you have a pendulum that may be dislocated by some exogenous, extraneous force but it will swing and, eventually, come to rest at the same equilibrium point.

Now, this is not appropriate because financial markets basically *discount* the *future*. However, the future that they discount is not something independent of their own discounting mechanism. Present decisions made in the financial markets actually shape the future, which the financial markets are supposed to discount. In natural science the connection between the scientist's statement and the subject matter to which the statement relates is one directional. The events occur independently of the statements you make about them. Therefore, you can establish universally valid laws, like equilibrium. In financial markets, and, generally, in human affairs, there is a two-way connection as the participants' views shape the events to which they relate. Since you cannot base your decisions on knowledge, you cannot rely on knowledge alone. You have to bring your own bias to it, your hunch, or prejudice, or whatever. That bias shapes the events, it does not determine the events, since you operate with *imperfect understanding*, your actions have *unintended consequences* and that is why you do not reach equilibrium necessarily. You have this two-way feedback mechanism, which I call *reflexivity*. That is reflexivity, which gives you a *historical process* where you do not return to the point from where you started, and this is more appropriate for understanding financial markets than equilibrium.

When I wrote the "The Capitalist Threat" article in 1997, I did not expect to have a practical demonstration as soon as we have now with a crisis, which has started in Thailand and reverberated around the world. Instead of financial markets acting like a pendulum, they are acting more like a racket ball that has knocked over one economy after the other. So financial markets are inherently unstable. If *financial markets* are *inherently unstable*, then stability has to be an objective of public policy. In practice this has been recognized because the development of capitalism has been a continued series of crises, each of which, then, led to some new form of institutionalized regulation. This is how central banking and regulations of stock markets have developed. However, the institutional framework for dealing with financial crises is basically organized on a national basis and since financial markets are global, you now have a hiatus, a *lack* of *adequate international mechanisms* for maintaining stability in the financial markets. That is a very acute problem. Of course, you have the Bretton Woods institutions, which are international institutions, and they have adapted themselves to changing circumstances. Of course, the national authorities have collaborated and continue to collaborate in trying to preserve stability. But obviously it is inadequate and the current crisis has clearly shown the inadequacy of the approach. Part of it is due to this false view of financial markets which actually also penetrates into the thinking of the financial establishment, the IMF, and the national authorities.

The main lesson to be learnt from the Asian crisis and from the inadequacy of the intervention is that there is an asymmetry in the actions of the monetary authorities and the IMF. They are basically there to protect the system. In the time of crisis, they do actually bail out the lenders or the investors who have taken unreasonable risks. They impose conditions on the countries that got into trouble. They basically impose a medicine that is designed to enable those countries to fulfill their obligations. That is why maintaining a stable currency is a top priority, because that makes it possible for the country to meet its international obligations. Actually, the countries that did not buy the IMF's medicine did rather better than the ones that did in this case. In the future, there ought to be a better balance in the regulatory intervention between imposing conditions on the debtor countries and also imposing conditions on the lenders and investors. While people are now criticizing the IMF for interfering too much, I criticize the IMF for *not interfering* enough.

Now I come to my second point concerning the relationship between *capitalism* and *democracy*. In my opinion, we actually do need democracy to make capitalism stable, because we *need* a *social counterweight* to offset the excesses of capitalism, even to maintain markets. Since competitors are not there to preserve competition, they are there to win in the competition and if they are successful they eliminate competition. They create trusts, or monopolies, or oligopolies, and interfere with free competition.

We need democracy as a counterweight, but with the development of global capitalism the power of the state to intervene in the economy has been greatly reduced. That is one of the merits of global competition. But it is also one of the dangers. I am certainly not an advocate of state intervention in markets. However, you need then some international institutions to preserve market stability. Even the institutions that we have are currently endangered because of the belief in market fundamentalism, which is quite strong at the very center of capitalism, in the USA.

What needs to be done to correct these excesses? Purely on an abstract level, this is where I would like to re-introduce or reformulate the concept of *open society*. The global capitalist system, as it currently functions, is a distortion of an open society. It is very close to an open society, it has many of its features, many of its advantages but the belief in individual decision-making is carried to an unsustainable extreme. In the past, when Karl Popper explained the concept of open society and when he engaged in a very profound debate with Friedrich Hayek, who was also a believer in an open society but at the same time he was an apostle of laissez faire, at that time the only danger to open society was from totalitarian ideology that would use the power of the state to impose its will on the people. Today I think we have to go back to the epistemological basis of open society, which is the recognition that our understanding of the world in which we live is inherently imperfect. This is the concept of fallibility. Just because state intervention is flawed, it does not mean that markets are perfect. There is a greater danger at the moment from *unhindered capitalism*, or unconstrained capitalism, for the preservation of open society than there is from state intervention. That is really the point that I was trying to make in my article.

Once we recognize that perfection is unattainable, that we cannot have equilibrium or perfection of any kind, we have to be content with the second best, an imperfect society that we are determined to try to improve and, since it is imperfect, the *scope* of *improvement* is *infinite* because perfection will never be attained. That is the concept of open society. Guided by this concept, I think we could develop institutions which would make *capitalism more stable* and also perhaps *more equitable*.

Andrew Brody:

George Soros' paper reviews our present experience and knowledge concerning the intricate *balance* of *freedom* and *order* in human society. It has an avowedly utopian character. But a world that has no blueprint of how to improve matters is not worth living in.

The general trend of Mr. Soros' argument is compelling. However, the domain it covers is much broader than a mathematical economist can face. Thus, I have chosen two topics for closer inspection. The first is about *equilibrium* in *economics*. The second is the problem of the *enemy* of the *open society*.

Most of the markets are not reflexive and most of the capital is not electronically transferable. I, therefore, propose a different approach to equilibrium. It leads to the same conclusion: a troubling *volatility* of the *markets*. What is this approach to equilibrium?

Mainstream economics, even in its most sophisticated form, like Professor Lucas, maintains that the economy is mostly in equilibrium. As a natural reaction to this, there comes up an opposition, of Mr. Soros, of

Professor Kornai, asserting that the concept of equilibrium is hollow, meaningless, because we do not find the economy in equilibrium. But there is a middle point worked out by John von Neumann and implemented by Wassily Leontief, which maintains that the existence of equilibrium does not require a convergence to equilibrium. Indeed, Neumann defined equilibrium in a mostly *thermodynamic* way as maximizing something and minimizing something as a saddle point. It is very difficult to investigate it and even with new statistics and the methods given by Leontief we can only approximate it.

What will happen if the equilibrium point is not an attractor? More or less the actual situation will fluctuate around it, cycle around it. Indeed, there are as many *economic cycles* in our system as there are products. It so happens that one of the most important equilibria, monetary equilibrium, which was already approached by Keynes, happens to fluctuate with a 200 years long swing. This means we had it in Europe, those four cycles ending with monetary revolutions. Since it goes hand in hand, and probably the precursor of the monetary revolution is a revolution in communication systems – the speed of money depends on human communication – therefore those four great cycles which we had in Europe and which according to my latest computation also happens now in the United States are 200-year cycles and if David Hackett-Fischer is right, who investigated those price cycles more closely, we happen to be on a threshold, a crisis point, a critical point with an inflation which is much faster than the inflations which connected the former four plateaux of the scholastical, renaissance, enlightenment, and capitalist system. Is it good or bad? I think it adds a new dimension of freedom noticing that we are in a crisis, noticing that our present decisions will shape the structure of the next two hundred years.

There is no way to do anything against the *200-year cycle*. It is relatively easy to smooth a little bit a four-year or a ten-year cycle because faster cycles have lesser energy. But already with a 200-year-long cycle, a government has not enough money to do anything against it and, very interestingly so, a monetary cycle is a strictly human business. We humans are entirely defenseless against it. It ravaged, transformed already four times the shape of human society. Now that means that we are near a catharsis and I read Mr. Soros' paper as a very good sign of this *catharsis*.

The market system is very good for goods that are freely reproducible and David Ricardo really started his system as a science about freely reproducible goods. We now notice that there are *goods* that are not freely reproducible; money is one of those things because it is a monopoly. Clean air resources, clean water, our surroundings and creative thought are not freely reproducible goods but they too are afflicted with equilibrium quantities and equilibrium prices. They are not very happy with it because it is not a good situation. Therefore, I used the word "afflicted." But they do have a price and they do have an equilibrium quantity around which they fluctuate.

The *existence* of a *general equilibrium* is warranted. This is important because in lack of its existence economic life would be totally chaotic. If this equilibrium is a strong attractor, a so-called focal point, then freedom would suffer, being reduced to the freedom electrons or chemical substances possess. Thus a certain balance between freedom and order is preconceived in our social relations.

Now what does it mean? Is our system strictly speaking periodical? Are there strict returns? No, because there are so many cycles that absolute return takes aeons. As Mark Twain said: "History does not repeat itself but it rhymes."

The point of economic equilibrium is not a simple maximum. It is a *saddle point*, minimal for profits, maximal for growth. This antagonistic principle, the *min-max criterion*, is essential for the movement around equilibrium.

Now what is the meaning of a saddle point? That there are *countervailing forces*. If there are no countervailing forces, if a government wants to maximize its profits and its growth at the same time, then it can achieve temporary miracles, but its stability will be lost. This is because the speed of growth on the true equilibrium path, though the fastest in the long run, can always be surpassed in the short. Thus growth can always be boosted in a given direction for a while. But the drive along other directions cannot be sustained for long. The faster path becomes less and less clear and transparent, the overall economic situation blurs and the economy runs awry. The "big jumps" invariably end, like the Soviet system did, in a quagmire.

An *enemy*, that is a free counter-agent seems therefore *necessary* for economic equilibrium to exist at all. Therefore, the main danger to the open, free and progressive society is not capitalism as such, but the lack of a countervailing force. With the Soviet debacle, the capitalist system became immensely proud albeit the failure of its antagonist did not improve anything in the system itself. A really important message for the open society is that all those forces which want, by collusion or corruption, to harness the countervailing forces will necessarily perish because it endangers this very intricate balance between freedom and order which mankind has to forge out for the next 200 years.

Olivier Giscard d'Estaing:

I think that capitalism is the worst system except all the others. You remember, Churchill was saying that for democracy. I will try to challenge Mr. Soros a little bit. I do not think that there is a capitalist threat. The threats our societies are facing are others. We have to fight against the threats but it is not capitalism. What are the threats: the scale and the speed. We call it *globalization*. It is a tremendous change in our daily life. In the financial markets we have trillions of dollars moving around the world. We have products and information going all over the world. This creates a new society, which needs new structures that are absolutely consistent with the capitalist system, which I will try to demonstrate.

Take *speed*. We are informed each minute about what is going around the world. The pace for the life of products has immensely increased. Products have a very short life. All these constraints certainly require new thinking, new approaches not to become victims. We have losers. Those losers might be countries, provinces, corporations, individuals, all those who are unemployed, because we cannot use their talent in our societies anymore, those who are left over. So we have to combine the creation of wealth and the distribution of wealth and the market. Of course, it cannot do it by itself unless there are certain rules and certain behaviors.

Capitalism for me means four things: *fair competition*, *private ownership* of the *firms*, *proper state* and *international regulations*, and *proper behavior* of the *actors*, professionally and ethically, whether they are public or private. I think you can forget about the concept of laissez faire. It does not exist. Not even in the USA. You know very well that there are antitrust laws, so many regulations that the lawyers are making fortunes. I agree: in France, in Europe we have too many regulations. But at least each one of them has certain objectives. For me the *regulations* would have two main objectives: one is the *environment* and the other is *solidarity*. So the question is not to have no state intervention or all state intervention. The problem is to have intervention for what purpose, how much, how it is being decided, how it is being applied. These can be worked out very well.

We did not want a free trade area at the level of the united Europe. We turned down the British offer and we wanted a common market, which means that we are going to agree on our rules of conduct. We are going to try to adjust our social policies, our fiscal policies. So the companies are not going to pay for the discrepancies among our structures. Now we have moved to the point where we will have the common currency, which will need an international authority to make it workable.

The second level is the globalization of trade, investment, communication, and technology. The figures are fantastic. The three hundred largest companies control 25% of the world, 20 trillion dollars stock of productive assets, and their sales are over one trillion dollars, which is 20 percent of the world added value. The crossborder financial flows exceed daily one trillion dollars. This is absolutely unregulated and, thus, it is wrong. We need to have control of those movements. James Tobin suggested that we would tax a small amount on that money and apply it to social needs, fighting against poverty, and all the diseases of the world.

When we created the IMF after the war we wanted to have a world central bank, which is not the case. The IMF has very little power. The countries where the IMF does not intervene are better off because, of course, they are working well. The IMF comes only when there is a trouble. The only problem is that IMF has no power of decision. So we have to balance the sovereignty of a nation and the international rules making the world properly working because we are all interdependent. So my proposal is that we should strengthen all our world authorities, the World Bank, the International Monetary Fund and the United Nations and their agencies. I am closely working with the World Trade Organization. Within this organization we try to anchor an evolution of the different markets so we have this fair competition I am mentioning. We are working with the International Labor Organization to avoid child work, because I do not call it fair competition to have your product, which is made by unpaid people or by children competing with our own products. We have to reach *international agreements* on these matters.

My last point is probably the most important and it deals with *human behavior*. Since finally we are all actors. It depends on our own attitudes and understanding of our profession and of our general interest. I am, therefore, surprised that we all speak about financial markets all the time and very little about human capital which is much more important than the money. According to Gary Becker, 75% of added value is coming from the man, not from the equipment. This is really the creation of wealth. You should try to have a vision of developing a society. You have to include your philosophy of developing man, to explain his role in today's and tomorrow's society, his contribution and what he will take. It means also *ethical values*.

I do not think that profit and money is enough as a motivation for a man or for a society. I am always shocked when you say that capitalism is to make money, profits. No, no. I am for the profit. We need to have individual and collective motivation to do what we want. But don't forget that in France at least we pay three times our taxes, taxes on dividends, taxes on private income and taxes when we purchase a good. The redistribution already in France amounts to more than 50% of our GDP that is a large amount. But, again, I think we probably have to include this into a *new philosophy* of *capitalism* by thinking that capitalism, if we make it work with proper attitudes and proper institutions, will be our great hope for the future.

Ferenc Rabár:

There are several ways of *criticizing* a socio-economic system. One can criticize the economic theory behind the system. It is possible to criticize the assumptions on which the economic theory is based, and there is a possibility to say that reality has changed and the system that we deal with is already functioning in a different way, so it is not the original system anymore. Mr. Soros has used all the three arguments in his article. As to the *theory*, he says that laissez faire ideology, which he proposes to call *market fundamentalism*, is just as much a perversion of supposedly scientific verities as Marxism-Leninism. This rejection is based on the denial of the *assumptions* of the theory. Perfect knowledge, homogenous and easily divisible products and the large number of market participants so that no single participant can influence the market price, are all assumptions that we do not meet in reality. Though neither of them applies to the real world, especially the first is emphasized. According to Mr. Soros the shape of the independently estimated supply and demand curves incorporate expectations about events that are shaped by those expectations.

The bulk of the criticism is based on the *changed reality*, on the collapse of communism, on the overall globalization and on the changed environment of the open society to be built. The changed environment from this point of view means: that the totalitarian threat gave way to the threat of laissez faire capitalism, on the one hand; and that however imperfect the open society is, it became global, but as such it is threatened by selfish individual nation states instead of excessive individualism, on the other hand.

Society is the key word we have to turn to and here is where we seem to find the first contradiction. Soros does not seem to realize that open society and laissez- capitalism have grown from the same philosophical roots. Hayek remained consequent and faithful to these roots. He was fanatically against international aid given to the poor. He was against redistribution, against solidarity. Hayek was consequent. However, I think Soros is right. Society implies redistribution, justice, co-operation, and communication. The existence of society cannot be separated from the *existence* of *common good*.

We have to know that libertarians have a different picture about society. According to Mrs. Thatcher, "there is no such thing as society. There are individual men and women and there are families. No government can do anything except through people and people must look to themselves first." John Stuart Mill says, "The initiation of all wise and noble things comes and must come from individuals." Yet this was not the original classical thought. Amartya Sen refers to Adam Smith who emphasized in his *The Theory of Moral Sentiments* that humanity; justice, generosity, and public spirit are the most useful qualities for society.

Kenneth Arrow demonstrated that in order for a competitive equilibrium to exist, each person must prepare a complete list of all future states of the environment, which might be obtained. The individuals make decisions in a world where uncertainty prevails. As Paul Ormerod puts it: "we have an economic system in which individuals at the micro-level are learning their own collective macro-behavior, which latter is in turn the result of micro-behavior. The behavior of such systems at the aggregate macro-level cannot be deduced from simple extrapolation of the behavior of a single individual. The whole is different from the sum of the parts. There *is* such a thing as society."

The open society of Mr. Soros is based on this conception. He accepts that "there are some shared values that hold society together." While maintaining individual freedom, tolerance and the promise of fallibility, he did not draw the extreme societal consequences from the neo-liberal ideas. Thus he was forced to confront with the extreme economic consequences of the same ideas.

I see the main problem of the paper where it deals with the changed international relations. Here I think a much more sophisticated approach would be needed. In the paper he simply *substitutes* the *selfish individuals* by *selfish nations* and the common good of a nation by that of the global open society. The scene is much more complex. National governments, multinational corporations, financial capital and wage earners have changing roles and different interests in this world. Their behavior, their fights, their clashes lead to a lot of old and new questions in economic theory.

International economics is out of date; it is *inadequate* to deal with the new problems. Questions like the following ones should be answered: Will the present mobility of capital lead to a global equilibrium or to a general exploitation of labor? Outsourcing and extreme mobility of capital: do they substitute the politically determined immobility of labor? How long is the present capital-labor substitution possible without reducing the effective demand on the market leading to stagnation and general economic crisis? What will be the result of national antitrust laws and anti-monopolistic regulations going hand in hand with an unconstrained freedom in the international field? How do the winner-take-all markets work? Robert Frank and Philip Cook have recently written about them. Boris Becker, Carl Sagan, Gabriel Garcia Marquez, Gerard Depardieu, Mel Gibson, Gary Casparov, Stephen Hawking, Andrew Lloyd Webber, and George Soros are mentioned as examples of people who work on these markets which are very different "from the ones economists normally study."

Jörn Rüsen:

The point of George Soros' *criticism* of *capitalism*, of what he calls now market fundamentalism, is that he looks into the internal structure of this system, finds problems, thinks about the solution of the problems and by doing this he transgresses the realm of economy and finally comes to the field of humanities and philosophy. Soros has delivered a very subtle argumentation concerning the *reflexivity* of *economy*. I would say reflexivity could be called *history*, because history exactly is a temporal change of the human world, of the specific kind Soros is emphasizing.

The second field is *politics*. Asking for international co-operation raises the question of politics, which goes beyond economy. The question that democracy has to counter-balance capitalism leads from capitalism into politics because you need *extra-economic criteria* to keep the economy running according to its own objectives. The same is true for society. The issue of society – as Soros says in his paper – is that without a certain feeling of the people belonging to a community, without an anchor in society we cannot even think of people doing proper economy.

The last realm is philosophy. Here the issue of principles or values is raised. Karl Popper has elaborated the vision of the open society in a critical turn against totalitarian systems. Now the totalitarian system has vanished. Popper's vision has to be reformulated. We do not need any longer the criticism of something, which does not exist but a perspective into the future of the system, which has survived. That can only be realized in going some steps further into the issue of values guiding politics, social life and, of course, the economy. Now we are in the realm of culture. So without a certain cultural condition, the capitalist threat cannot be met and the future of the free world can't even be designed in an intellectually responsible way.

Let me just enumerate three problems that we have to face and solve. The first is the issue of *identity*. Identity, personal and social identity, is a necessary cultural condition for a kind of economy we all are thinking about and pleading for. That is a question of the *roots* of *values* in the minds of the people. Here we have to think about memory, historical consciousness, and history as a cultural phenomenon that roots people in their social context and enables them for an activity in accordance with the value system we are speaking about, mentioning fair competition and proper behavior. Identity is brought about by certain cultural practices.

The second issue is *universality*. We have a tradition of these universal values that play a decisive role in anchoring human life in social context and bringing about a stable identity of ourselves. The best examples of this system of universal values are the *human* and *civil rights*. But even the system of human and civil rights is structurally insufficient. They have an unsolved problem concerning the social preconditions of citizenship, as long as labor is a condition for civility. This is an open problem because we can observe a world wide growing unemployment. That means a systematic deprivation of social conditions for political citizenship.

The next issue is related to the *environment* because it is a hidden implication of the idea of human and civil rights. Here human subjectivity is defined by a specific relation to nature. It is the relationship of exploitation by labor. That has to be reformulated since it has catastrophic consequences, if our exploitative treatment of nature simply goes on.

But there is another problem, which is the most urgent, at least in my view. It is the problem of *cultural difference* vis-à-vis the universality of our value system in the globalization process and vis-à-vis the universalization of the Western style of economy. Today there is a strong debate between the universalists on the one side and the culturalists on the other side. Culturalism is a problem and not the solution of Western intellectual dominance. The solution will be that we have to establish cultural practices of *intercultural communication,* which are based on universal values and at the same time, acknowledge and recognize cultural differences. If this could be brought about, then the globalization process would include the globalization of some features of the Western civil society, which has lost its threat to the non-Western people in the globalization process. A universalistic idea of mutual recognition of differences is the solution of this problem, and it can dissolve the threat to the non-Westerners of a Western cultural imperialism. Here the humanities play a decisive role, because it is up to them to bring about a convincing idea and an effective practice of intercultural communication in which this mutual acknowledgement of differences is realized. The next step will be to implement this idea in the minds of people by education and cultural practices. If that could be done, human beings would not only become agents of a capitalistic market, but they will become independent citizens of a new world order based on human and civil rights which are complemented by the universal right of acknowledgement and recognition of cultural differences.

George Soros:

There is no tremendous controversy among us. So we have to develop some of the ideas further rather than to engage in a sort of fight against one another. Basically all the speakers were developing the ideas rather than contradicting them. To some extent they were contradicting. Mr. Giscard d'Estaing was saying that there is no such thing as a *laissez faire* economy. That may well be true. The criticism was raised that the percentage of GNP in the developed world that is in control of the state has not varied very much. In fact, it has grown; it has doubled since the end of the Second World War. So where is this laissez faire capitalism? I think that the laissez faire ideology, what I now call market fundamentalism, is very much a driving force. There has been a tremendous change in the role of financial markets, the freedom of capital to move, and the relationship between labor and capital since 1980. So I would dispute that there is the influence of market fundamentalism, which is today a dominant influence. In that respect, of course, France is fighting a rearguard battle trying to maintain state control, the welfare system, and is, in fact, being overwhelmed by international competition.

As far as Mr. Brody is concerned, I am not so sure about the 200-year cycle. But there is very much a long-term cycle and it is not a complete cycle. I do not see history in terms of periodicity because each cycle has some similarities and some differences. Certainly, the so-called *Kondratief phenomenon*, the long wave cycle that is, he says, 50 years, I think it may be a little longer. That is very much a factor taken to be account and we now have a very interesting phenomenon emerging particularly in Japan where conditions resemble those that Keynes was dealing with. John Maynard Keynes has fallen out of favor because, in a way, he was too successful in curing depression. Fiscal stimulation and fine-tuning created inflationary pressures. So that led to a swing back to controlling the money supply and to monetarism. Keynes was dismissed. I think Keynes lives again because in Japan you see conditions of excess capacity and insufficient demand. You see the pushing on the string that Keynes talked about. The pushing does not actually bring about a stimulation of the economy. Here the cycle comes back.

But I thought the most interesting aspect of the contributions was to deal with the second part of my critique: the need for a global society and for *globally shared values* to sustain a global economy. I, of course, agree with Jörn Rüsen that reflexivity is history. That is, in fact, my point and I regard financial markets as a historical phenomenon rather than a mechanical phenomenon in the manner of equilibrium and eternally valid laws.

Rüsen raised the question of global identity. Yes, we need to have some common, shared values in order to have a global society that makes the global capitalist system workable. As he also said that we need to have those *ethical values*. Can we develop them? I think that fallibility could be the basis on which such values can be agreed on, but it really does have to be elaborated. I am very worried about the concept of global open society because I am trying to elaborate it actually, but it is very abstract. How is it going to be accepted? How is it going to be translated into something that a large number of people can agree with? Generally speaking, to create common ground you need an enemy. Look at me, I have selected *market fundamentalism* as my *enemy*. So it is what I consider to be the main problem that somehow we need to overcome.

I do not think that we can have a global government, it is just simply not in the cards, and there is no support for that. In fact, the existing international institutions work very badly, and have been discredited. I am talking particularly of the United Nations. Here we have to go *beyond economics* and to look at *politics* and security issues.

International institutions generally do not work because they are associations of states and the national interests; the interests of states generally take precedence over the so-called common interest. Of course, we have one very promising development and that is the European Union where a smaller group of nations has, at least partially, in the economic sphere subordinated, and surrendered its sovereignty to a central organization. In that sphere, it works reasonably well. But, for instance, in foreign policy, which was the second pillar of the Maastricht Treaty, it does not work because the states have not surrendered sovereignty. Now Europeans have the creation of a common currency, which is a wonderful step forward in forging the unity of Europe, but it is a tremendously risky proposition because Europeans now have a common currency without a common fiscal policy and it will prove to be unsustainable.

Either the European Union will move forward and will take another step towards creating some kind of a federal structure or the whole edifice may actually collapse under the strains. So it is a very risky situation. But at least in Europe, there is something to move forward. But on a global basis it would be a complete utopia to talk about. However, I think that we can set up *specialized organizations* for *specialized purposes*. For instance, stability of financial markets, a clear and present need, could be addressed by changing the mandate of the IMF. I think if we have organizations, which have a mandate, they are more likely to succeed than, for example, the UN, which basically is an association of states where the states do not surrender their national interests.

Unfortunately, the USA has suffered from a crisis of identity since the collapse of the Soviet system: there was an enemy that allowed the USA to be the leader of the free world and one of the two superpowers. Now we do not have that opponent anymore, so we do not know whether we want to be the superpower or the leader of the free world. Thus, there is a great resistance to build genuine partnerships. We can see the tensions in situations like dealing with Bosnia and Kosovo. The USA actually despises Europe for its inability to act in unity. It is not totally without justification, because in fact there has not been a united Europe in foreign policy. Thus, we are dealing with a great number of divergent interests and they are in conflict with one another. If the Western members of the UN Security Council had been able to agree, they could have prevented the Bosnian tragedy. Thus, in the end, the USA more or less went for it alone. However, it has left a bad legacy. So, this is where, I believe, the real problem lies: to forge a *coalition* based on *common principles* that could even make the UN a more effective organization. Then, hopefully, we would have a majority of democratic states that would run the organization, rather than just do it on a strictly proportional basis.

Olivier Giscard d'Estaing:

In my view our public opinion and our politicians are not ready to go for a world government and the United States is not willing to accept it. Look at the way they play with the UN! I know they do not like the principle of one-country-one-vote, which is not good indeed, but we still have the small Security Council and all the means to act.

You may find it funny, but I like the prospective approach to the future. I have written a short story about the first world president, who is fifty years ahead of us and who happens to be Hungarian. I am going to make a Jules Verne prediction ahead of us: we will have one world currency. It sounds incredible now, but we are going step by step towards it. We will have the Euro and the dollar. We will also have a currency for Asia. Then those three currencies will establish relations among themselves without too many variations in order to have a stable world currency system and we will come to a World Bank. This is my vision, but nobody believes in it now. Maybe one century later they will remember our discussion and think that we were right.

The world currency and its necessity will create the power to control it. This is what is happening to the European power. Mr. Soros says that we are not united, well; we are united as compared with where we were fifty years ago. I was in The Hague fifty years ago when I heard Churchill saying that we need a united Europe and we have done it. We have made a great progress. I believe that the *European social model* is the model of the future where we assume responsibility towards those who need it. It all depends on how far one can go. France probably went too far, but we will react by the adjustment to the Common Market. We are obliged to do that in order to compete. We are going to fight against what we call social dumping which means that low salary countries will finally win the competition. Low salary countries that will develop will increase their wages and their social protection to near our model. I still believe in what Henry Ford said: "Give them high salary and you will have a strong economy!"

Jörn Rüsen:

There are some basic issues to be dealt with. One is the issue of supranational power. I agree with Mr. Giscard d'Estaing that Europe is already a paradigm for that. It is easy to despise the Europeans for not being able to send an army quickly to some places in the neighborhood. But on the other hand, it indicates a complete lack of aggressiveness of the united Europe. That is an advantage. What we need is a counterbalance to organized aggressiveness on the one hand, and we need some supranational power to keep up peace on the other hand. As a historian, I must say that we should not forget that the Europeans had to pay a very high price for their unification, namely two world wars with millions of victims.

The other issue is that in the long run there will be one world currency, the *Mondo*, as we can call it. From the Euro to the Mondo. My point is that we should not only look at money, currency and capital but also at the same time at *culturally conditioning forces*. Thus we have to ask for a culturally conditioning force of the Euro. Let me come back to my favorite example, namely the system of basic rights. We have a European set of basic laws, and we have a High Court, which enables every citizen of the EU to sue his or her own government to this Court. The government obeys to the decisions made there, which is a form of supranational, cultural guarantee of civility, a part of a very complex system of interrelationship between culture, economy, society and politics. The same has to be applied to the Mondo. We have to work out this system not only for political institutions, which have the ability to enforce, for example, the rules of a fair economy, but at the same time we have to make efforts to enlarge it to world culture.

As to identity, we cannot have a universal identity because identity is always something particular. But we can use universal values in order to create an *open-minded*, particular *identity*. This is only possible if we bring about a structural shift in the cultural practice of creating identity. The traditional cultural logic of creating identities is ethnocentrism with a clear distinction that here we are and there are the others and we need an outside enemy. Now in the globalization process we have to take steps towards a new cultural strategy of creating identity. Let me say it is a turn from the logic of exclusion to the *logic of inclusion*. Then, the enemy is a part of oneself and that changes the whole attitude in the relationship between one's own self and the otherness of the other.

George Soros:

One of the unfortunate side effects of our open society and marketized society is that people actually lose their identity. They need to re-establish some kind of identity and it does not have to be an open-minded one. I mean that there can be nasty people in the world as long as you have got some institutions that maintain law, order and peace in the world.

I would like to make a point about the imbalance between the center and the periphery in the global capitalist system. There is a definite imbalance: the center is the provider of capital and the periphery is the user of capital. Just as there is an imbalance between the position of financial capital and labor, there is also an imbalance in favor of the providers of capital as opposed to the users of capital. Unfortunately, at the present time it is reinforced by the way the IMF operates which then imposes conditions on the countries without demanding some contribution from the investors. I cannot tell you how the Multilateral Agreement on Investment (MAI) would affect this imbalance, whether it would correct it or not. If it merely opens up markets for investment, it will not do so. You need some measures to correct it. Right now there is a lot of investment in emerging markets, partly because of the imbalance, and when things really go wrong you get bailed out. Thus, heads you win, tails you do not lose very much. That was the case in the 1982 crisis as well as in Mexico. If that is the spirit in which the MAI is going, it will not solve the problems.

Andrew Brody:

Mr. Soros is not convinced of the 200-year cycle, but I guess it does not mean that he denies that again for some decades the return on capital surpasses the rate of growth in the USA or the world at large. For the present, however, it means that he does not consider the depth of crisis deeper than the downswing of Kondratief and the might of transformation not stronger than usual.

George Soros:

No, not because that would imply a periodicity. Since I consider that history follows a *unique path*, I do not exclude any depth to which we may fall in the current cycles.

Olivier Giscard d'Estaing:

The Americans and the Europeans shall reinforce actions towards the rest of the world, because we have common grounds and common power in order to do it and we should do it in a new approach. We have one enemy in the world and it is *poverty*. On the side of poverty everything is merging to destroy our societies. Look what is happening to the Islamic world. The Islam is not very dangerous in the rich Islamic countries, but where countries are poor, like Algeria, the Islamic grounds and the hatred that comes towards the richer countries, is a source of great worry for the future.

Ferenc Rabár:

I think we have heard a lot of optimistic and pessimistic views. The capitalist threat does exist and we have to deal with it and continue this kind of discussions.

Jörn Rüsen:

The situation is ambivalent. Capitalism has to go on in order to overcome poverty, for instance. At the same time it has to be humanized. That is a challenge and this point came out very clearly during our discussion.

George Soros:

In no way should my critique be misread as a condemnation of capitalism, of internationalism, of cosmopolitanism and so on. The instabilities and inequalities of the capitalist system could feed into *nationalistic, ethnic* and *religious fundamentalism*. It is exactly why we should prevent a return to that kind of fundamentalism by *correcting* the excesses of *market fundamentalism*.

Ethics of Capitalism

Peter Koslowski
Hannover Institute for Philosophy
Germany

"Morality of an economic system" looks like a contradiction in terms, a *contradictio in adiecto*. The economy as the system for the provision of material goods ought to meet economic, not moral norms. For the sake of the efficient production and distribution the economy even ought to be kept free of well intended, but hindering, moral reasoning. These postulations, however, already imply an "ought," a counterfactual, normative element. The economy itself is not an "ethical neuter," since it is not only determined by economic laws, but also by humans whose will and choice are guided by a combination of manifold expectations, norms, mental attitudes, and, last but not least, by moral conceptions. Human action ensues from highly complex conceptions, economic reasoning forming just one part of them.

The way of looking at the economy as at an autonomous social system is of modern origin and has become apparent only since Mandeville. (Dumont, L. 1977) In traditional, premodern societies economic action is inseparably connected with religious, family, and political action. It is not until the rise of capitalism that the economy becomes an autonomous sphere of society. Is this process a process of liberation, a process that can be justified in moral terms, or is it a process of dehumanization and alienation? Marx interpreted this process as both liberating and alienating. According to him capitalism destroys all "feudal, patriarchal, idyllic relationships," but on the other hand capitalism, and capitalism alone, has proved, "what human activity is able to bring about and has achieved miracles totally different from Egyptian pyramids, Roman aqueducts, and Gothic cathedrals. [...] All that is corporative and fixed is vaporizing, all that is sacred is desecrated, and men finally are forced to look at their situation, their mutual relationships with sober eyes." (Marx, K. 1848. p. 464) So if capitalism is not only an economic, but also a social phenomenon, the question of its morality has to be trailed beyond the borderlines of individual ethics and can be met only by a holistic view.

The question of the morality of capitalism cannot contribute an additional moral aspect to the economic, sociological, and political aspects of the topic of capitalism; rather, it must be understood as the integration and moral evaluation of the totality of arguments. Morality is not one aspect among others, but a way to appreciate the perspectives and arguments of the sciences, to order and evaluate them, and to render them meaningful for human action. (Spanemann, R. 1980, pp. 39–40) The question of the morality of capitalism cannot be: "Is capitalism moral?" Rather, the question must be: "Is capitalism justifiable under the conditions of human nature and the scarcity of resources?"

A principle of the moral theology and natural right of the Baroque period stated that moral obligation arises from the nature of the object. (Molina, L. de 1602) The morality of capitalism can be justified only by the nature of the object, that is, the function of the economy and the possibilities it offers for human self-realization. Morality amounts to appropriateness to the matter and cannot consist in the abstract opposition of a moral ought as against economic arguments. As the distinction between descriptive and prescriptive propositions was never fully maintained and an economic natural right of efficiency always prevailed in economics, the question of the morality of capitalism need not fear the naturalistic fallacy because this objection has in some sense itself proved a fallacy. The moral inquiry is not opposed to economic theory but must take up the latter and ask whether all aspects of reality are done justice.

To the understandable objection that this claim to a totality of perspectives in ethics is very extensive, one must answer that people raise the question of the justification of their actions and of the system in this universality and not as an inquiry into single aspects of their existence. In addition, one lives in a totality of social conditions and is determined by them. One would want neither to live in a just society where there is nothing to buy nor in an efficient, rich society that employs its resources for morally reprehensible purposes. In the inquiry into the ethics of capitalism and into the totality of its characteristics, therefore, scientific precision must not be paid for by the renunciation of the entirety of possible aspects. At the same time it is evident that a social order can never be justified once and for all because the number and importance of the viewpoints by which it must be evaluated constantly change with time.

1. Conception of the Market Economy

In general, theories of capitalism are economic and not philosophical. The distribution of labor in the sciences has the result that the economists deal with the economic substructure and the philosophers with the superstructure of ethics and values whereas an integrated overall view is missing. This narrowing of perspectives leads to serious gaps in the theory of the capitalist society.

Within economic theory two approaches to the theory of capitalism can be distinguished: first the mechanistic model of general equilibrium in neo-classical economics and secondly the model of interaction in the Austrian school of economics. Hutchinson distinguished between a "Smithian" and a "Ricardian" foundation of market economy. (Hutchinson, T. W. 1979, p. 433) The Smithian tradition formulates social theories in a broad perspective including the political, legal, and ethical framework of the market, whereas the Ricardian tradition analyses the social problem in a narrow economic perspective and emphasizes aspects of efficiency of an utopian optimism that require complete anticipation.

Typically the neo-classical model can be interpreted as a mechanism that leads to the equilibrium if allocation is efficient. The efficiency of the allocation of resources for the satisfaction of existing demand stands at the center of attention. Since freedom leads to the greatest total benefit, all obstacles to freedom have to be eliminated, but if this allocative optimality is disturbed, other efficient modes of allocation have to be found.

Thus the market, as Buchanan put it, is turning into a "mechanism, into a calculating machine that computes information and receives input or transforms output," a mechanism that, if it is disturbed (market-failure), is substituted immediately by other mechanisms of allocation like the state or voting. (Buchanan, J. M. 1964, p. 219., Koslowski, P. 1982)

On the other hand, in the "Austrian" tradition the market is a context for the interaction of acting individuals pursuing their individual ends. A context that mediates the individual persecution of objectives with those of all others and is thus facilitating freedom as the ability to act according to self-determined objectives. Next to the aspect of an optimal allocation the aspect of freedom is gaining importance. As Buchanan writes:

> The market or market organization is not a means toward the accomplishment of any thing. It is, instead, the institutional embodiment of the voluntary exchange processes that are entered into by individuals in their several capacities..., it is a setting, in which we observe men attempting to accomplish their own purpose, whatever these may be. (Buchanan, J. M. 1964, p. 219)

According to Hayek the market is that process of discovery in which we first experience what our objectives are and which resources are scarce. (Hayek, F. A. von 1968, p. 7. and 9.) Correspondingly representatives of this tradition are more readily prepared to stick to the market as an instrument of allocation even when forced allocation might be more efficient.

The problem of the ethics of capitalism arises within the economic theory in the openness of the system, in the possibility of a trade-off between efficiency and economic freedom. (Rowley, C. K. & Peacock, A. T. 1975, Dupuy, J. P. 1978) The model of general market equilibrium has no unequivocal, automatic solution but rather remains dependent – because of market failure in the case of externalities, indivisibilities, and so on – upon the meta-economic determination of the optimal relation between freedom and efficiency.

The model for the mechanism of choices leaves open in the last analysis a non-mechanical grade of freedom. How can one achieve a balance between freedom and efficiency in the economy? According to J. Marshak, "the sacrifice of liberty is an organizational cost." (Marshak, J. 1974, p. 199) However, this does not advance the inquiry as to how this sacrifice of freedom is to be evaluated. This question remains one of a balancing between social values, which transcend the purely economic model.

One cannot immediately switch to forced allocation at every disturbance of the optimal conditions nor can one, as K. J. Arrow correctly objects, hold non-interference to be the only value. (Arrow, K. J. 1967, p. 12) The science of choice, welfare economics, is of no help here either as the discussion of the possibility of a social welfare function has shown. (Buchanan, J. M. 1969, pp. 62–64) A mechanical solution of the overall optimum is not available.

F. H. Knight has critically examined the mechanistic analogy in economics. The general equilibrium model interprets economic behavior in accordance with the analogy of force in which the motive causing an act is understood as force. (Knight, F. H. 1935, p. 241) Economics must then be concerned with actions arising from preferences that are not further questioned. The Newtonian concept of force in mechanics has been criticized in physics as metaphysical by E. Mach and H. Hertz, but it acquires justification insofar as forces in nature and observable and experimentally reproducible. That is not the case, however, for economic preferences, which are conceived as forces behind the choices of individuals.

Preferences have a primarily social character; that is, they are influenced by social status, training, and education, as well as by error. Preferences and choices are not identifiable like force and the effects of force in the natural sciences. Market competition cannot be considered according to the model of force and opposing force, which lead to an equilibrium of forces. The mechanism model takes goals, motives, and the preferences of individuals for the given and only accepts considerations as to means. It is a model of adaptation in which the individuals' acts of choice are based upon their unquestionably accepted preferences and the force conditions of the market. No value problem concerning the selection between goals in accordance with certain categories arises in this model.

2. Morals in Capitalism

Through the acceptance of given, constant goals, the moral problem is reduced to an economic one, and ethics is replaced by economics. Knight sees this "displacement of ethics by a sort of higher economics" in classical economics and in utilitarians like Bentham and J. S. Mill (Knight, F. H. 1935) It also appears in the case of Spencer. Looking at contemporary theoretical discussions one could see socio-biology and bio-economics as attempts to introduce a universal economics. For utilitarians, who are thoroughgoing hedonists, well-being is the goal of all action. Ethics is then reduced to the optimal allocation of resources for the goal of the greatest pleasure. This goal is empty and formal, and as long as the substance of pleasure is not determined, the maxim of maximization of pleasure means no more than each doing as that person wishes anyway. No help in making selections can be drawn from the concept of the greatest pleasure or utility. On this basis, the individual cannot choose if he does not already know what he wants. The "economy of pleasure" leaves the individual helpless if he did not know already at the beginning of his cost-benefit-analysis what kind of pleasures he is striving for.

Among the objections to hedonism that have been raised since Plato are that people do not want pleasure or utility but rather seek concrete goods and that they do not desire plain pleasure but distinguish and rank various pleasures.

Thus, Plato argues in *Gorgias* that a person interested only in satisfaction should best wish himself an itch, so as to be better able to scratch himself. Max Scheler further criticized hedonism by saying that one cannot attain happiness immediately but rather obtain it "on the back of other activities." (Scheler, M. 1966, p. 351) One does not play the piano in order to be happy; rather, one can be happy when one knows how to play the piano. One's interest in capitalizing precisely does not obtain the goal when one does not do things for their own sake.

Knight raises against hedonism the old philosophical and religious wisdom that suppressing desires instead of trying to satisfy all of them may lead to a greater degree of happiness and is definitely more economical. (Knight, F. H. 1935, p. 31) Finally, in accordance with Alchian, it can be referred to the fact that under conditions of a complex environment of an action and of uncertainty about the strategies of the others, utility maximization cannot be considered as an operational advice of action since the individual cannot find out which of all possible courses of action is exactly utility maximizing. (Alchian, A. A. 1977, p. 17)

The two approaches just presented, that is, the elimination of ethics from capitalism by means of the mechanism model and the attempt of utilitarianism to make economics into a kind of higher ethics, share the intention of reducing incommensurable preferences and needs to a common denominator. Within the mechanism model this is effected by having recourse to constant motives as the relevant acting forces, which reduce the problem of choice to a problem of adaptation, within utilitarianism by tracing back all motives of action to the formal motive of utility maximization.

Both approaches are attempts to avoid the value problem inherent in the selection among goals by using tools of economic theory. Thus, "economics might almost be defined as the art of reducing incommensurables to common terms. It is the art of heroic simplification." (Shackle, G. L. S. 1972, p. 10) Both positions amount to the attitude correctly described by K. E. Boulding as "knowing the value of nothing and the price of everything," which means nothing other than that the economy can show the individuals the relative prices and the optimal allocation of their resources for certain goals, but cannot relieve them of the choice between goals and values. (Boulding, K. E. 1967, p. 67)

A. Formation and Co-ordination of Preferences: The Coherence of Ethics and Economics

Preferences are not rigidly given and invariable, and the social problem is not merely one of economizing the use of means. Preferences are ethically and socially transmitted; they are formed in individual ethical reflection as well as social interaction. Symbolic interactions, as was presented by G. H. Mead and W. I. Thomas shows how closely one's view of the world and one's perspective is determined by groups and communities. (Knight, F. H. 1935, p. 129) One sees goods not in themselves but rather in a close weave of perspectives of different reference groups to which one belongs and in the symbolic definitions one gives to the qualities of the goods.

According to the *Thomas theorem*, symbolic definitions of situations that people adopt are real in their consequences. From this point of view, culturally defined needs are as real in their consequences as physiological needs. One can consider needs as constant only in abstraction and in the very short run. De facto, preferences continually change by way of the transformation of institutions and society.

As deliberation upon the correct allocation of resources for given purposes, economics can provide information on the possible extent and opportunity costs of the fulfillment of goals. However, Knight points out that it can "never get beyond the question of whether one end conflicts with another end and, if so, which is to be sacrificed." (Knight, F. H. 1935, p. 37) In the case of a conflict between competing goals one must abandon the level of scientific economics and use preference rules. Ethically speaking, the question as to which goals an individual in a society sets for himself is more important than the question of how this goal is to be fulfilled.

It is obvious that the ethical and sociological theory of the formation of preferences is logically prior to economics as the theory of the allocation of resources for these preferences. One must ask about the reasonableness of the goals *and* about the optimal allocation of resources for these goals. Neither of these questions can be reduced to the other. Society is not conceivable as a pure *katallaxia*, as the problems of a Paretian social overall optimum show. With a given factor endowment and given preferences, a condition is conceivable in which the complete variability of all quantities and of the anthropological presuppositions for the indifference curves leads to a situation in which no one can improve his or her position without another being hurt. Can this be interpreted as a real optimum? Let us set aside the problem of the initial distribution of endowments for the moment. It is still apparent that all adaptations in the system are more or less of a strategic character. Preferences were not examined or transformed for rationality or goodness but under the assumption that they are fixed and given merely adapted to variations in the environment. The Pareto-optimum cannot, therefore, define social or ethical optimality beyond the economic viewpoint of allocative optimality.

The ethical postulate must still be raised that individuals should vary their effective demand not only according to their own given preferences and accommodate to those of others in the course of exchange in such a way that a Pareto-optimal position is reached, but that they should *transform* their preferences in an ethical way respecting the preferences of others. They should not only move on the indifference curve but change their system of indifference curves at times.

K. E. Boulding claimed that every movement on the indifference curve to a point on the contract curve presupposes a certain indulgence and the absence of jealousy or envy. If one follows this thesis, the Pareto-optimum implies a moral minimum. Yet such a moral minimum in a Pareto system cannot be an optimum in a moral sense. (Boulding, K. E. 1973, p. 113, Doi, T. 1973)

It is an underestimation of ethical reason and a scientific fallacy to assume that people only *adapt* their preferences *strategically* and are unable to *transform* them with respect to the totality of conditions. The model of the market and the Pareto-optimum acquire an ideological character when they are presented as the last word concerning the theory of action.

This is even more so the case with respect to attempts, by way of a recourse to socio-biological and bio-economic categories, at saving *economics as the universal science* in view of the objections of anthropology and sociology which point to the cultural and institutional formation of preferences and choices. For example, J. Hirschleifer after having conceded that man being "full of love and hate and sheer cussedness ill fits to the model of economic man," introduces the economic gene in order to save the universality of economics. (Hirschleifer, J. 1978, p. 240) The gene directs the choices of man so that he produces or promotes identical duplicates of his genetic equipment.

Clearly, the interest of the social biologist is to eliminate acts of choice in a strict sense. No longer the man but rather the economic gene is the doer behind the deed who attempts to strategically secure identical copies of itself. Here the choice between competing values is eliminated; there can no longer be any choice between conflicting goals. The unitary goal of nature and society is simply given and all actions are merely strategically resisted to it. Apart from the animistic element in this theory and the conflicting empirical fact that with sinking birth-rates especially wealthy societies do not contribute to the maximization of identical gene copies, although they could do so best, the theory of socio-biology presents the most reductionist interpretation of the value problem. However, socio-biology, contrary to its critics' assertions, is not a theory of capitalism since capitalism does not restrict itself to purposes of genetic reproduction but rather admits all individual purposes biological, economic, and cultural.

The value problem in capitalism arises because it is not centrally predetermined, and individual evaluation of goals, that is, freedom, is held to be a value. Freedom is both a fact – as non-intervention – and a value category. (Knight, F. H. 1947, p. 4. and 372) It can be seen as an instrument for reaching other goods as well as being a value in itself.

The understanding of freedom as pure non-interference with market forces eventually leads to a pure mechanism in which everything that occurs without political intervention appears to be good. This understanding of freedom can be seen in Spencerism and social Darwinism. In western societies, freedom, understood as the ability to act according to self-chosen goals, is seen as an intrinsic value, which has pushed other values, such as stability, calculability, and personal continuity into the background. The concept of freedom is bound up with the dialectic of freedom and self-responsibility, without which a free capitalistic order is unthinkable. This burden of freedom brings about the fact that a free economy cannot be, as it were, derived from efficiency criteria, but rather presupposes a moral will to freedom. Freedom and property must be wanted, as an act of the will. (Röpke, W. 1949, p. 280)

The value of freedom as an intrinsic good comprises a certain fixed relationship to other values. They ought to be able to be valid only if they are freely affirmed by the individual, and only in the case, where the possible coexistence of the values that the individuals set for themselves is guaranteed.

Capitalism as the system of contractual labor relations and free entrepreneurship excludes the finalization of the economic process according to centrally set goals, that is, the household model of the economy. It does not eliminate the problem of value; it rather puts the burden on the individual. Economic individualism therefore, is, necessarily tied to ethical individualism.

The problem of economic individualism is the following: What must I do in order optimally to reach my goal under the given constraints, and under the condition that others pursue their goals? The ethical problem is: What should I want? What are reasonable preferences? The answer of ethical individualism is outlined in the *Critique of Practical Reason* by Kant, who must be considered the founder of the philosophical ethics that correspond to a market economy: "So act that the maxim of your will could at any time serve as a principle of universal legislation." This ethic corresponds to the structural characteristics of capitalism: individualization, autonomisation, and universalisation. (Koslowski, P. 1982) It is, as in the case of a catalytic economy, not finalized but mediates between formal and individual goals. It attempts to provide a criterion; according to which it can be determined whether or not one's individual goals are compatible with those of all others. If the individual goals pass this test, on the next level the question arises: How can these goals coexist with each other in the reality of the economic sphere?

The same objection to Kantian ethics has been made as was raised against the Pareto criterion. It is not capable of providing an answer to the basic problem of practical philosophy: What should we do? The categorical imperative is more a criterion of negative rejection than a procedure for the selection of goals.

One cannot live without values as criteria for deliberation between alternative courses of action. In this case, the bounds of rule-directed, methodical thought appear. The good can neither be determined solely as universalisation nor expressed as a single category of value. In the selection of alternative forms of action one remains tied to the totality of the situation and of value categories, and one must treat the situation for action as a whole. It is one of the basic insights of philosophy that the good cannot be expressed in a single principle or value, but rather it must be determined as the totality of aspects of a situation and the nature of the matter. The idea of the good, according to Plato, cannot be presented as one single principle but rather as *truth*, that is, as the emergence of that which a person or a thing can be if it realizes the possibilities inherent to its nature (*aletheia*), as *beauty*, and as *measure*. Such a notion of the good certainly invokes methodological objections from a scientific point of view, to which Knight replies: "This is of course intellectually unsatisfactory. The scientific mind can rest only in one or two extreme positions, that there are absolute values, or that every individual desire is an absolute and one as 'good' as another. But neither of these is true; we must learn to think in terms of 'value-standards,' which have validity of a more subtle kind." (Knight, F. H. 1935, p. 40)

The difficulty of making such an ethic of the balancing of the totality of aspects operational puts quite a burden on the moral imagination of the individual, but the ability to deceive oneself as to possible relevant aspects of an issue to be decided is one of the characteristics of the immoral. The obligation to consider the totality of perspectives can compensate for the lack of operationality by the absence of a dogmatism of rules and a better consideration of possible side effects. (Churchman, C. W. 1961, Simon, H. A. 1978)

B. The Need for Business Ethics

Especially within capitalism leaving a large space to individual freedom, there is the need for an ethic of the economy and of business that integrates the totality of value perspectives into the positive and normative analysis of economic choices. The need for a business ethic cannot be denied by contending that there is an automatism of competition.

The belief in market automatism is expressed by the frequently heard proposition that the market is not reconcilable with non-economic, ethical rules of behavior. The dogmatic belief in the forces of market competition can be best illustrated by W. J. Baumol's dictum that the market cannot sustain a non-economic ethics and that the automatism of competition renders an ethics of business superfluous. (Baumol, W. J. 1975) Under the conditions of perfect competition, voluntary moral acts of a single entrepreneur – such as ecological measurements, training for handicapped, and so forth – are not desirable for Baumol since the moral entrepreneur will be thrown out of the market within a short time. According to Baumol, "The merciless market is the consumer's best friend." Voluntary supererogation only hurts the single businessman. Baumol asserts that social measures should be enforced by government on *all* firms: Firms should not be "all-purpose institutions, but make money for their stockholders. [...] The notion that firms should by themselves pursue the objectives of society is, in fact, a rather frightening proposition. Corporate management holds in its hands enormous financial resources. [...] I do not want management to use the capital I have entrusted to it to impose its notions of international morality on the world." (Baumol, W. J. 1975, pp. 46–47)

Baumol's dislike of moralizm in corporate management derives from an unjustified optimism about the functioning of the mechanism of competition. Only if all firms produced on the break-even point and there were no producer rents, would every producer who fulfils supererogative actions be driven out of the market place. This case is very unlikely. Producers who produce with costs below the break-even point can afford moral voluntarism very well. In oligopolistic markets, managers can trade off slack for profitability. (Williamson, O. E. 1977, p. 188) They can choose between an easy life for the management and profit maximization. Therefore, they can choose between slack and moral actions as well. Baumol's position shows the fallacy of the mechanistic model. In reality, the alternatives for actions allowed by the economy are much more complex than the classical cost minimization or profit maximization model suggests. Economic practice always takes place in a social totality in which the consideration of additional aspects of economic action, which transcend the model of economic man, is not only moral but can be profitable as well. Moral actions can have spillovers in profits.

There is a certain irrational passion for dispassionate rationality in the economic theory of capitalism, which bans any kind of moral motivation or thinking in terms of values from social science. It endangers the conditions of conservation of economic rationality. (Weisskopf, W. A. 1971) As an example take A. A. Alchian and H. Demsetz's theory of the entrepreneur as the monitor of firm members' shirking: "Every team member would prefer a team in which no one, not even himself, shirked. Then the true marginal costs and values could be equated to achieve more preferred positions [...]. Obviously the team is better with team spirit and loyalty, because of reduced shirking – not because of some other feature inherent in loyalty or spirit as such." (Alchian, A. A. & Demsetz, H. 1977, p. 101)

Here the economist's belief in what Dennis Robertson calls the "need for economizing on love" goes too far. Critique of ideology adopts an ideological character itself when it denies the intrinsic value of moral action or constructs an opposition between morality and advantage, which ethical theory always has doubted. The ethics and particularly the natural right tradition has always – with the exception of Kant – claimed that there is an accordance of morality and *enlightened* self-interest. This accordance has recently even been confirmed by economic theory.

Sauermann and others have proven that trust reduces bargaining costs. (Sauermann, H. 1978) J. M. Buchanan shows that ethics is a substitute for the direct control in large groups where this control would be costly. Ethics is designed to solve the large number dilemma. (Buchanan, J. M. 1965, 1978)

As Sen has demonstrated, the general belief in ethical norms can solve the isolation paradox that each person would do (the) good if he knew that the others would do so as well, but will not do it if he might be the only moral individual in the group. It changes the prisoner's dilemma into an assurance game. (Sen, A. 1967, 1973)

Arrow interprets moral codes as reactions of society to the rise and for the compensation of market failure since moral codes can lower transaction costs and thus leave everyone better off. (Arrow, K. J. 1971, p. 22)

E. C. Banfield shows that the absence of trust and social integration and the predominance of non-enlightened self-interest is an obstacle to economic growth. (Banfield, E. C. 1958, p. 89) A generally accepted business ethics lowers the transaction costs of market interactions. Transaction costs cause the shift of transactions from the market into firms, which form internal markets for labor and capital (m-form structure, holding corporation). These internal markets are more integrated than the general market by corporation-specific behavioral codes (corporate ethics, corporate philosophy). They increase the conformity between firm members' actual and expected behavior and reduce transaction costs. (Williamson, O. E. 1977, 1981)

Even the mechanistic model of general equilibrium theory of neoclassical economics does not render ethics as the trans-economic evaluation of alternative actions superfluous. To decrease transaction costs, moral rules ought to be made generally binding and be internalized by the market participants. Micro-economic theory shows the need for a business ethics and for reembedding business, the market and the economic motivation into ethical and social norms. Thus, the structural characteristics of capitalism should be reembedded in the ethics and culture of a society.

3. The Morality of Capitalism and the Limits of Its Justification

According to R. A. Posner, "in a world of scarce resources, waste should be regarded as immoral." (Posner, R. A. 1977, p. 23) Posner's statement could be read as a tautology with which everybody agrees: Waste is a pejorative notion, and no one would call waste moral. In the context of positivist economics, however, this sentence stands for a tendency to regard the allocation problem as the only ethical-economic problem since ethical judgments concerning goals are considered unscientific. In this perspective, capitalism would be the most moral system since it undoubtedly solves the allocation problem with the least waste as compared to other systems. Nevertheless, one cannot stop asking questions at the point of the allocation problem as has been demonstrated in the discussion of individual ethics.

A. Selectivity of the Market and Distributive Justice

For a justification of capitalism, the distribution resulting from an optimal allocation of resources must be investigated, as well as the question of whether capitalism selects or filters out certain goals in the market process. The apologists of capitalism have continually attempted to evade both questions by representing allocation and distribution as simultaneous processes (marginal productivity theory) and disputing the selectivity of the market in pointing out that everyone, according to his willingness to pay, could realize all of his goals in the market. Both arguments are correct but not the whole truth. The arguments are connected. It is correct that allocation and distribution must go together, for otherwise there would be no incentives for an optimal allocation. Moreover, the positive contribution of a productive factor to the total product is one criterion of just distribution, and the consumer's willingness to pay for a given good is *one* standard for the intensity of preference. Goods should go to those who desire them most intensively, and because this can hardly be determined other than through willingness to pay, therefore, to those who are prepared to pay the most.

A competitive market does lead to the employment of every productive factor when it can bring forth the greatest product, measured in prices, and leads to a distribution, which reflects productivity and relative scarcity. This argument from efficiency is not a sufficient ground for the morality of the distribution, which results from the remuneration according to the marginal productivity of a factor of production. Even if the problem of economic computation could be solved, the problem of moral computation would remain.

All property rights on resources, whether labor (human capital) or capital in general arise from three sources: effort, inheritance, and luck. (Knight, F. H. 1935, p. 56) Of these, only the first source can doubtlessly be called just, the second is merely legal, and the third incommensurable with justice. Thus, the distribution, which arises from these three factors, cannot be considered moral in an emphatic sense, but only be considered not immoral. Scarcity rents stand for the accidental characteristics of the distribution in the market process. Certain factors are scarce, given to their owners only by an accident of nature, yet are in demand. Other factors are just as scarce but not demanded. Is this sufficient reason to justify the enormous difference in distribution between both of the owners?

Hayek's and R. Nozick's approach that the distribution must be accepted as the result of a game that proceeds according to impartial rules and cannot be manipulated leaves the moralists unsatisfied and cannot even please the players. (Hayek, F. A. von 1977, Nozick, R. 1974) After a certain point in time each game requires a new dealing of the cards, a re-creation of the same initial conditions. For the game of life, which we can only play once, this must be even more true.

A continual, periodic equalization of the initial positions is for reasons of efficiency not possible and criteria for such a distribution are lacking. Natural differences cannot be redistributed. But one cannot, as Nozick has suggested, disqualify every conception of end state in a theory of justice with reference to the rules of the game. That would be the capitalistic reversal of the dictum, let justice be done, though the world perish (*fiat justitia, et pereat mundus*), into the principle that the rules of the game must be obeyed, even when the chances in the game are very uneven, and even when the end results can be predicted and are trivial.

A purely deontological entitlement theory of justice is as abstract as a consequentialist theory of end-state justice that continually shapes society in accord with its image of end-state justice. Hegel's remark in his *Philosophy of Right* on ethical principles applies to both: "The principle of scorning the consequences of action, and the other, of judging actions by their consequences and making them the standard of what is right and good are both abstract understanding."

The unquestioned acceptance of the primary distribution which results from the market in capitalism without giving consideration to the final social effects of the effects of the economic process is no more moral than an arbitrary redistribution that is continually reshaping society and economy according to a prefabricated image of social justice.

Since distribution and selectivity of the market are correlated, both problems reinforce their respective advantages and disadvantages. An economy solely grounded on marginal productivity and effective demand results in an unequal distribution and means that the wealthy succeed better in enforcing their goals in the market. Nevertheless, this inequality can be compensated for by the fact that the consumer needs of the lower income classes become more homogeneous and, therefore, can be satisfied at lower relative prices if in the production of mass goods economies of scale appear.

Problematic, however, is the position of the consumer in the market who has a low income and particular or even extravagant preferences. He will find himself in the position described by Werner Sombart: "What use is it to me if I am a friend of hackney cabs, or of stove heating, or of silent film? I do not have any other choice but to consume automobiles, or central heating, or sound film, or – passive resistance." (Sombart, W. 1937, p. 16)

The same is true for the position of those producers who have a valuable good to offer for which there is, however, no effective mass or elite demand. The extremely subjectivist theory of value, which would hold that under these conditions the good in question is not really a valuable good, ignores the reality of the market, which is always determined by the whims and ignorance of the public. (Knight, F. H. 1935, p. 57)

Especially in more egalitarian capitalist countries where certain cultural goods have not been reached by the public demand yet, and where those classes which so far have made possible the production of certain superior goods by their higher willingness to pay are due to this legalization not able to do so anymore, a specific form of market failure may result. This is true, for instance, for certain technical and craft abilities, which have been driven out by the industrial mass production. Already at the end of the eighteenth century, defenders of the guild system like Schlosser have pointed to this process of driving out of crafts by industrial mass production. (Schlosser, J. G. 1787)

Industrial mass production and the buying power of the majority taste cause an egalitarian tendency in capitalism that is often overlooked – despite all attention to developments in income distribution. It causes a tendency for the assimilation of equal life-styles behind the unequal income distribution. This tendency stands in contrast to the fact that one of the main and correct arguments for capitalism is that it makes individual life-styles and ways of life possible to an extent no other economic system did or does. (Macrae, N. 1981)

Consumer sovereignty and the direction of market production by subjective preferences and effective demand causes the Janus-headed character of capitalism between egalitarianism and luxury and between freedom from domination and the oligopolistic power of the big firms. The fixation of prices according to demand and supply only removes all feudal privileges and causes a sociological equalization. On the other hand, it sets preferences and demand free of all social restraints or aesthetic criteria and allows parvenu luxury just as well as personal austerity. The market removes social barriers, on the one hand, and creates economic inequality, on the other hand, by the enormous accumulation of wealth as rewards for successful innovations or as quasi rents.

The tolerance of capitalistic societies toward the accumulation of wealth and the lacking embeddedness of wealth in ethical or social norms is certainly one of the critical points of capitalism. It makes the need felt for a new awareness of legitimacy and social obligation among the economic elite.

Economical inequality raises the question of power. To what extent are individual preferences effective within societal and economic decision-making processes, how far are these processes distorted by economic power in favor of certain groups? In order to answer this question, it would be incorrect to compare the really existing, imperfect markets with ideal, perfect procedures of democratic participation. Only realizable conceptions of decision-making processes may be compared to each other.

With respect to the problem of power, Buchanan has referred to the structural relationship between the market and voting, that is, between the dollar vote and the equal right to vote at the ballot. (Buchanan, J. M. 1954, Buchanan, J. M. & Tullock, G. 1962)

Markets and democracy both require that decisions be made on the basis of individual preferences. As the Condorcet–Arrow paradox has shown, the market or the dollar vote is much more successful than voting in doing so. The market can register the intensity of preferences which are expressed by the individual's willingness to pay, and it forces the individual who must cast the dollar votes to a greater expression of his or her preferences and to greater responsibility in his or her decisions. The market increases by its continuity and non-restrictedness of decision alternatives the individual's chances to participate in decision making.

B. Limits of Subjectivism in the Theory of Values

Nonetheless, there remains a feeling of moral dissatisfaction with the market mechanism that cannot be explained merely by the inequality of the initial distribution and, therefore, by the greater choice possibilities of inherited wealth. For the market to be moral and the point it chooses on the production possibility frontier to be reasonable, would require that the effective demand, that is, the preferences of consumers were moral and their knowledge perfect. No one could assert that the choice decisions in the market are on the whole ideal or reasonable. Too much nonsense, bad taste, and superfluous luxury win out over necessary, meaningful, and beautiful goods.

In addition, not only are given preferences co-ordinated and streams of factors directed through the demanded production of goods, but new needs are created through the market as well. As Knight points out, "The economic system forms, transforms, even creates wants. An examination of the ethics of the economic system must consider the question of the kind of wants which it tends to generate or nourish as well as its treatment of wants as they exist at any given time." (Knight, F. H. 1935, p. 46) The moral guilt for many nonsensical needs is not to be borne alone by firms, which want to introduce new goods, but rather by the drive to imitation and the prestige needs of consumers.

It is thus rather remarkable that the proponents of economic democracy criticize the capitalistic system. For if consumers are incapable of asserting their sovereignty as consumers who are opposed to commercial advertising, they cannot begin with the presupposition that the choice makers in a democracy would be able to maintain their choice sovereignty with respect to political advertising in a plebiscitary democracy. Both kinds of "people's sovereignty," the sort of consumer sovereignty which is detached from all religious, aesthetic, and moral norms in a market system which is *solely* oriented toward subjective needs and the sort of political people's sovereignty detached as well from all norms in a plebiscitary democracy without constitutional norms, are equally a cause for fear.

The market system has always brought forth the criticism from religious quarters, which expressed the opinion that the market system gave too much room to human irrationality and overly trusted the ability of human reason. In contrast to the interpretation of Edward R. Norman and J. V. Schall, according to which capitalism is conceived upon a pessimistic anthropology based on original sin, the conception of a subjectivist and domination-free market represents the result of an optimistic, enlightened anthropology. (Norman, R. 1979, p. 10, Schall, J. V. 1979, p. 37)

One cannot dismiss the religious critique as paternalism. As Max Scheler asserted, "We all believe either in God or idols." (Scheler, M. 1966) When the religious formation of preferences is abandoned, other forces for molding preferences, other Gods or idols appear.

A pure catallaxy is an ideal of co-ordination but not a meaningful social program because one does not come into the world as a freely decision-making being and utility-maximizing economic (hu)man, but is rather subjected to the influence of the environment and of the social reference groups to which one belongs. One needs the institutions and the action-directing norms just as much as, occasionally, paternalistic direction. The theory of market failure and of free-rider behavior with respect to public goods shows this. A society built only on revealed preferences would not be a nice place in which to live.

When under certain conditions the methodological individualism of the market leads to fallacies of composition, that is, the fallacy that what is good for the individual is also good for the whole, and then this should be true of the voting process as well. Under these conditions, nothing is to be gained by the transfer from the market to a plebiscitary democracy. (Koslowski, P. 1982, 1983) It is much more to be feared that the needs which are not fulfilled in the market (public goods, cultural goods, the environment) would not be properly considered in an ideal democratic process as well. A good portion of the critique of capitalism is equally a critique of democracy and a critique of the inability of individuals to make reasonable use of their consumer and voter sovereignty.

The strengths of capitalism, that it can admit of many goals and of many values insofar as they can be borne by the market and that it abandons the attempt to finalize social and economic processes, are weaknesses in the eyes of those who hold that the market does not properly deal with certain values. Criteria are, however, not available which would tell in which succession or in which intensity values and goals should be realized by the economy. Because freedom in the first place means the ability to set goals for oneself as Kant has demonstrated, one must concede to the economic actors the freedom to set goals for themselves even if one knows better in which order these goals should be realized.

Nevertheless, objections must be raised against the *value agnosticism* of capitalism which contends that one does not have available any criteria at all. Freedom cannot be the only value that a society can further. One cannot hold an allocation mechanism to be moral which, as Malthus writes, "denies a man a right to subsistence when his labor will not fairly purchase it." The justification for the non-finalization of the economy in wealthy countries can only go as far as the needs of subsistence have been secured.

C. The Significance of the Non-Finalization of the Economy

That capitalism, despite its successes, has such a bad reputation is to be regarded as a result of the not understood problem of the non-finalization of the economy. Almost every group considers its own goals to be insufficiently provided for by the market system because the goals of the market system cannot be fixed by the group in question. Farmers see their market results as being insufficient, as do artists and philosophers. That the intellectuals are especially active in the critique of capitalism is caused, as Norman has clearly shown for the English tradition of capitalism critique, by the fact that they view their goals as not being sufficiently encouraged because of the lack of mass demand for what they supply. (Norman, E. R. 1979) This is certainly the case for representatives of the social sciences. Capitalism with its trust in spontaneous, unplanned order offers them little opportunity for the implementation of their knowledge. In this respect capitalism contrasts with planned economies, which by definition must make the social planner the director of the economic process. The effects of this phenomenon on the income and wealth distribution are even favoring an increase of the critique of capitalism among the intellectuals and the intelligentsia.

It can not be denied, on the other hand, that capitalism also favors a certain group as far as the distributional results are concerned, namely, the group that fulfils best the conditions and expectations on which its economic system is based: the group of the successful entrepreneurs. Nevertheless, it severely punishes the same group if it does not fulfill the system's expectations: the unsuccessful entrepreneur.

Every conceivable system always favors the type that corresponds best to its definition. Planned economies favor the planner, theocratic societies the priest, and belligerent societies the military. Capitalism has here the advantage that the fulfillment of system and role expectations and the social and economic remuneration of the economic elite are fairly efficiently connected with the interests and needs of the population, that is, with consumer demand. The consumers' possibility for "exit" (Hirschman, A. O. 1970) in a competitive market and the control of profits by competition between producers assure to a certain extent that economic success and remuneration are linked to socially desirable and useful performance.

Against the critique of interest groups upon the allocation and distribution effects of a non finalized capitalistic economy, one must recall one of the oldest views of justice in the European tradition, the idea of equilibration and measure. (Koslowski, P. 1996) A society, which bases the pursuit of its goals on *one* normative principle only, or supports the purpose of only *one* group is not able to realize the good. (Fritz, K. v. 1954)

The idea of an equilibrated totality of goals and ends is an idea that must be aimed at the critics of capitalism as well as at those who absolutize the allocation mechanism of the market. The theory of market failure as well as that of government failure indicate that a balance must be found between society and state, market and voting. (Koslowski, P. 1982, 1987) Both the market mechanism and the state show their failures. The morality of capitalism cannot consist, as Knight has shown, in introducing abstract economics as absolute ethics, that is, in reducing all questions of social and ethical values to the question of the optimal allocation of resources for satisfying given individual preferences. (Knight, F. H. 1966) The totality of the social order must not be understood only as a market.

The moral justification of capitalism consists rather in mediating many goals and their pursuit by individuals in such a way as to preserve moral and economic freedom without a war of all against all. That which the individual and society takes to be preferred can only be reached by the market through a compromise between what the individual takes to be important and that what all others take to be important. A compromise is all that can be reached when individual pursuit of goals is allowed.

Competition in the market is and must be a competition ruled and limited by law. It is – using a risky paradox – a kind of institutionalized peaceful civil war. "In case it (competition) goes out, we are threatened with a kind of pensioner's existence at the expense of the state, whereas the external competition between the states persists. Terror fills this gap," Ernst Jünger asserts. (Jünger, E. 1952, p. 37) The terror of social determination of goals by *one* group is the alternative to competition in advanced societies because, according to historical experience, only through terror can a society which has experienced freedom be sworn to a particular goal. This interdependence has been proven once more by the experience of the East European planned economies.

4. Some Social-Philosophical Conclusions

A. Capitalism as Utopia

According to our knowledge of history, a purely capitalistic society, built exclusively upon private property, maximization of utility and profit, and co-ordination by way of the market and price system, has not yet been a reality. As a societal model, capitalism bears utopian, contractual features; it is itself a social utopia. Its utopian character always becomes evident when its defenders seek to immunize their opponents' objections with the incompleteness argument, that is, by pointing out that it has never been realized in its pure form and that its shortcomings can always be traced to exogenous influences. Such a procedure is not justifiable from an ethical standpoint. A social theory must adjust itself to reality and take its historical locus and historical conditions of realization into account. A theory that presents a superior model but can never be realized due to exogenous influences or non-producible preconditions is a bad utopia and remains in the "precociousness of the obligation" (Hegel).

As a theory of society, capitalism cannot suffice because it is essentially an economic theory of production, exchange, and co-ordination. As an economic theory, it must neglect essential aspects of social action and political integration. In this work, the omission of problems prevailing in many approaches to the theory of capitalism has been exhibited above all in the assumption of given preferences in neo-classical economic theory but also in the limits to the principle of co-ordination by markets. In both cases, the cause is to be found in an exaggerated methodological individualism and subjectivism, which assumes one can neglect the social mediation of one's preferences and the obligation to have reasonable preferences for the sake of individual freedom of choice.

By making freedom and efficiency the sole guiding values in its ideal of co-ordination, the theory of capitalism evades the problem of comparing goods and gains its most impressive comprehensiveness in general equilibrium analysis. The problem of weighing goods against one another cannot be avoided, however, as the problem of weighing sacrifices of liberty for the sake of increases in efficiency and vice versa demonstrate. This was already seen with the necessity of weighing efficiency against freedom in the selection of allocation mechanisms. The necessity of comparing goods also turns up in the preference formation of the individual, which cannot be regarded as a black box from which factual preferences pass into making a choice. The mechanism model of choice and decision making that interprets the actual choices and revealed preferences as the effects of inexaminable forces, the inner preferences, successfully avoids illuminating the "black box" that is the preference formation for the revealed preference approach. But precisely the preference formation gains significance when with increasing social wealth and material satiation the production problem becomes less urgent.

B. Freedom and Freedom of Choice

This satiation also demonstrates the limitation of a concept of freedom that understands freedom merely as freedom of choice between the greatest number of possibilities. Quite often it turns out that a growing supply of goods does not cause that one feels freer when one has greater possibilities of choice among goods. Rather, such situations of an oversupply of alternatives demonstrate that the marginal utility of freedom of choice is also decreasing. Too many possibilities is just as unpleasant as too few alternatives, not merely due to overburdening of decision-making and problems of cognitive dissonance after consumption decisions but because this concept of freedom systematically touches on only one part of what human freedom is.

Philosophical criticism caricatured the understanding of freedom as freedom of choice in the High Middle Ages with Buridan's ass, which starves because it cannot decide between two hay stacks of equal size, and, in Modern Times since Kant, as the freedom of a turnspit. Moreover, in the mechanism model of general equilibrium theory there can be no real freedom. The agent is determined by his preferences and mechanically adapts himself by his consumption and production decisions to the prevalent market conditions.

Against this conception of economic freedom it must be stressed that freedom primarily means the ability to act according to self-chosen purposes, and that the choice of these purposes or the formation of preferences must be understood as a self-choice, that is, a decision about one's own being and personality. It follows that the concentration of economic theory upon consumption and consumption decision as the purpose of human and, in particular, economic action is one-sided because the personality forms itself essentially in its action and creative occupation not in its consumption. This implies that an examination of the extent to which the constitution of an economy admits free action and self-realization cannot be based merely on freedom of consumption.

The indubitable superiority of the market as a means of co-ordination manifests itself here in that it permits individual pursuit of goals and self-responsible action to a greater extent than all other forms of co-ordination, in that *the market permits not only freedom of consumption*, but *also freedom of action* and *production*.

C. The Necessity of a Social and Ethical Framework for Capitalism

It also turns out that the maximization of profit and utility as the economic motive, and the free disposition over private property assume a characteristic abstractness when they lay claim to unlimited social validity. The maximization of profit and utility can only be admitted as motives under constraints; otherwise they reduce the wealth of human motivation to abstractions of rationality and ignore the social embeddedness of the pursuit of goals. The same is true of rights of disposition over private property. (Koslowski, P. 1995)

The co-ordination of individual actions in capitalism must occur within a social framework, which the conditions of this co-ordination – private property, maximization of profit and utility, and the market system – do not adequately determine, but rather presuppose. (Nell-Breuning, O. v. 1955, p. 111)

The limits of capitalism as a social theory are that the co-ordination ideal does not comprise the whole of a society's guiding ideas, that the medium is not the message, and that the form of economic action does not fully comprise the substance of one's social action. As a social theory, capitalism is *materially underdetermined* and incomplete. It must be complemented by a comprehensive social-philosophical theory concerning the framework within which capitalism can activate its advantage as a method of co-ordination, by a theory of the social genesis and normative justification of preference formation (social psychology and ethics), by a theory of the social institutions of which this framework consists (family, churches and religious communities, state), and by a theory of political compensation for capitalism failure (market failure, the limits of subjectivism, and consideration of substantial life interests).

The necessity of such a framework becomes evident in the dialectic proper to the three structural characteristics of capitalism. In all three characteristics a change-over from quantity into quality and from form into content is observable. The unlimited accumulation of private property leads, from a certain point of mastery of a market to a qualitative jump and to a problem of power. Unlimited pursuit of profits and benefits leads to a change-over into greed, miserliness and a loss in the wealth of human purposes. The co-ordination of production and the assignment of social status exclusively by way of market success, that is, successful anticipation of demand and willingness to pay, leads to an exaggerated subjectivism and the neglect of more substantial purposes.

The *form* of co-ordination by way of property, maximization of utility and profit, and the market cannot be the *content* of the social order and individual action, no more so than this form can be abandoned if freedom and efficiency in the economy are to be secured. The theory of capitalism requires a complement from social philosophy and a reminder that *reasonable preferences* must enter into the co-ordination. It also needs the reminder that capitalism lives from an ethos of freedom and work, which as a form of economic co-ordination it alone cannot bring forth and preserve. An ideal of co-ordination alone cannot do justice to our need for substantial life forms, just as, on the other hand, our need for the recognition of our subjectivity and freedom, in the economy as well, requires the capitalist form of co-ordination.

The text is a reprint of selected chapters of Peter Koslowski's book *Ethics of Capitalism and Critique of Sociobiology* published by Springer-Verlag in 1996. We would like to thank Springer-Verlag for granting permission to reprint some parts of the original publication in this volume.

Misunderstood and Abused Liberalism

Lubomír Mlčoch
Charles University Prague
The Czech Republic

My paper, I believe, can be instructive and inspiring for the discussion of ethics of capitalism. I express this hope in spite of the fact that I have a particular interest in the specific social conditions of the transformation of the *Czech economy.* Incidentally, misunderstanding of the liberal doctrine is certainly not the exclusive fault of the architects of Czech privatization. Our negative experience is a lesson to be learnt not only in the countries in transition but also in countries with stable capitalist system. The erosion of the *moral grounds* for the *market economy* is omnipresent. So, lessons from misreading of liberalism and the abuse of its doctrine might be useful everywhere.

Already at the start of the post-communist transformation American sociologist, Amitai Etzioni has pointed out the idea that the transformation process represents an immense social experiment that will test empirically the validity of mainstream economics. (Etzioni, A. 1991) This is why, I am sure, the Czech experiences can serve as one negative example and perhaps a warning for more developed Western economies.

I have presented my ideas about the close connection between the chosen strategy of privatization in the Czech Republic and the general "social ecology" for ethical business behavior several times. The first occasion was in 1994 in the conference entitled *Cultural Consequences of Transition* in Rome. (Mlčoch, L. 1994) The second occasion was the international seminar *Business Ethics in Eastern and Central Europe* organized by Hannover Forschungsinstitut für Philosophie in Marienrode in 1996. (Koslowski, P. (ed.) 1997). Finally, I had the privilege to present the keynote address to the *10ᵗʰ Annual Conference of the European Business Ethics Network* in Prague in 1997. (Mlčoch, L. 1998)

I have formulated the hypothesis that the principal sin of the Czech privatization process was an overly speedy rate of institutional change. I used the adjective "radical" to describe the liberalism of Czech provenience. Later on other adjectives have appeared such as "naive," "primitive" or "vulgar" Czech liberalism. My predecessor in the function of the Dean of the Faculty of Social Sciences of Charles University, the sociologist Miloslav Petrusek spoken about "the Marxist's vulgarization of Friedrich Hayek" in our intellectual milieu. The former Vice-President of the post-Velvet Revolution Federal Parliament Jan Sokol and former minister of education in a recent article even goes so far as to use the brutal accusation that we are faced with a form of "gangster's liberalism." Nevertheless, thinking about the proper adjective for my paper I finally combine the terms "misunderstood" and "abused" to describe Czech liberalism, by which I mean that one thing was the bad reading of the liberal doctrine and another one was the abuse of ideology by compact interest groups lobbying in privatization games.

For some years, the architects of Czech privatization and economic transformation have been commonly appreciated as "exemplary scholars" of Western neoliberalism and monetarism. The Czech path to privatization was sometimes as a model to be followed. However, in 1998 the Czech government has received a lot of bad grades at home and from abroad as well. The pendulum of time has radically swung from full reliance to a suspiciousness with regard expectations, and too high an optimism in the Czech Republic has been substituted by perhaps too black skepticism. What did really happen? Where are the reasons for this failure or crisis of reliance? I would like to demonstrate that this crisis resulted from the deeply misunderstood concept of liberalism.

1. The Timing of Institutional Change

The speed of all... was regarded as absolutely essential.
(Václav Klaus and Dušan Tříska in August 1994)

Festina lente!
(An old proverb from the ancient Rome)

The effort of the Czech reform's architects to be as fast as possible during the payless transfer of public assets to the citizens differentiates the voucher scheme from traditional ways of privatization. I called the Czech case the "short way" (Mlčoch, L. 1995a). Advocates of the "fast" or "short" way of privatization are apparently numerous: they include supporters of the "shock therapy" and some "evolutionists" (Grosfeld, I. 1994), "economic informatics" as for example Pavel Pelikán, the Czech economist living now in Stockholm (Pelikán, P. 1994). Naturally, I need not mention the architects of the Czech economic transformation as fundamental supporters of the "short way." I have chosen one of their statements as the entrance motto of this chapter.

As to the supporters of "long way," we can join here the Hungarian economist János Kornai, the French economist W. Andreff, economic sociologist David Stark from Cornell University, and W. Brus, an economist of Polish origin from Oxford. Naturally, the lists of names on both sides are not exhausted. Myself, I have been led by my institutionalist background and intuition not to succumb into temptation of the spirit of radicalism.

The "short way" means that the government effectuates the formal change predominantly of legal framework as fast as possible and in such a way starts the spontaneous processes of natural selection. This relatively short period of the change of legal institutions and of the initial distribution of public assets escapes from any regulation. It is an "inevitably dirty process" (I. Grosfeld) – the transforming society is passing through a "dark tunnel" at the end of which the reformers hope to find a light. By this light is meant the free initiative of the new owners and the belief in the self-purgative abilities and selection of the spontaneous market processes, generating so lacking and so needed economic information without which the process of "creative destruction" cannot be open. The pragmatism and minimization of moral dimension of the "post-socialist accumulation of capital" are connected with a conviction, that after the end of "pre-privatization agony" and privatization anarchy, the government ought to show with emphasis that the period of "Klondike" is over, and since this moment "private property is inviolable"...

The "long way" on the other hand means the belief, that privatization in the post-communist countries is an inevitably long time process, lasting perhaps for some decades – with the eventuality of one exception, that of East Germany. The government should have a concept for the policy of corporate governance and management of de-etatised state enterprises. It means that the government should not meddle into microeconomic choices of the companies, but only to discipline managers by managerial contracts and stimulate them to enhance the future market value of managed enterprises. The private sector should be growing by the gradual evolution "from below" and by "step by step" portions of state enterprises restructured and privatized "from above" in the traditional way. I use the conditional in this sketch of the "long way" as this strategy has not been chosen.

The terms "short" and "long" way could be misunderstood. I try to show that the chosen "short way" liberates fast the government from economy only in appearances and for this reason the "short way" means a sort of *pium desideratum*.

For John Nellis the efficiency outcome of privatization is conditioned by the simultaneous realization of five complexes of preconditions that are as follows:

(i) emerging market of managerial services

(ii) evolution of functional capital markets as a mean of the permanent pressure on the discipline of managers

(iii) functional and effective institutions of "exit," that is of bankruptcy procedures, liquidation and buy-out of enterprises (hostile takeovers)

(iv) absence of political interventions into the economic sphere

(v) practice of corporate governance in the exclusive interests of shareholders. (Nellis, J. 1994)

It is sure from the realized experiment of the Czech "short way" that the completion of these five preconditions will not take a shorter historic time but the time horizon possibly needs the realization of the "long way." The Czech economy acquired specific cultural and ethical features following "its own way." I have to say that these cultural and ethical specificities arising from the futile effort to realize the "short way" are rather negative.

2. Trade Off Between the Speed of Change and Business Ethics

There is a possible trade off between the speed of privatization (or any other institutional change), on the one hand, and the emerging business ethics and legal and economic order, on the other hand. I would like to show that the attempt to effectuate the institutional change in a fast way could destabilize society and economy, endanger order, and undermine moral standards in business. The lacking firm and enforceable "rules of the game" in a hurry of the speedy social transformation is the consequence of misunderstood liberalism.

The speed of change can also cause the merely formal character and superficiality of the new institutional framework, and in the so-called "*recombined*" form, the old dysfunctions of the former regime are reproduced on the principle of "*path dependency*" (Stark, D. 1996). The two factors together can result into some special continuation of the social schizophrenia of the past regime, characterized by a sharp discrepancy between declared ideology and really exercised economic policy. The effort to unmask this schizophrenia belonged to the constitutive features of my descriptive analysis from inside of "real socialism" (Mlčoch, L. 1992b).

So, I affirm that penalties for getting over the reasonable speed have to be paid not only in road traffic but also during economic transformation. The traffic cannot work without clear and enforceable rules – the same is necessary for emerging capital markets. Until now theoretical economists calculated the social costs of the gradual way of transformation and argued with populist's threats of the slow-down in privatization. This point of view has been born from the illusion advocated by the radical liberals and neo-classical economists, namely that fast institutional change is possible in principle, and it is absolutely necessary for the effectiveness of transformation.

The privatization process in the post-communist countries cannot be a symmetrical institutional change to the original nationalization. So called "theory of the transient period" in the Marxist political economy of socialism has been the true "shock therapy" and it meant the forced change of the whole institutional framework of economy during a relatively short historical period. In our country, the historians of the planning system are in accordance that the new framework of the centrally planned economy was practically done at 1953, i.e. it had taken only five years since the communist "revolution" and mass nationalization decrees.

It was interesting and symptomatic that for the architects of the Czech transformation it took again only five years to declare that privatization is almost completed (in 1994). In the same way as the former socialist Czechoslovakia has been proud of reaching the highest ratio of nationalized sector among socialist countries (full 95%), the Czech Republic was said to get the first at the privatization milestone – at least in political declarations.

"*Time is money!*" sounds the well-known proverb relating at the most general level the time dimension of our dealings with the value equivalent of economic system. "*Lacking money takes time*" is my inverse formulation of this relation for the social task of economic transformation. Institutional change and restructuring are the immense social investments towards the regular market economy. As to the reasons for the strategy of fast privatization, it is possible to formulate a hypothesis that the reasoning was not only a matter of the pure economic theory of neo-classicism, evolutionism, or theory of economic information. The arguments came also from the political area.

The political markets are imperfect, as Douglass North has emphasized: political leaders have to provide a vision for the people with the promise of feasibility of the vision in a relatively short time horizon. The attempt to fulfill this promise leads to the ideology of radical, misunderstood liberalism. In this context, the Czech "short way" shows clear features of the "spirit of revolt" (Arendt, H. 1961) repeatedly emerging from the past (Mlčoch, L. 1992a). The protagonists of radical liberalism founded their vision on the shining shop windows of our western neighbors and on the promise of the fast way to this desirable world. For this drawing a thick line under the past was necessary and – "having a clean table"- the reform architects tried – as fast as possible – to make an institutional Xerox copy of the legal framework well-tested in the western market economies and to organize the redistribution of public capital assets into private hands, also as fast as possible. Unfortunately, the Czech government did not succeed in this institutional Xerox: the *standard market economy framework has failed*. Nevertheless, for a considerable part of Czech population, this attractive ideology has remained a kind of substitution for religion.

The "shock therapy" in this version is like a neo-classic analogy of all the former attempts at "great jumps," previously inspired by the Marxist ideology. The effort to cancel the past and to start with the *tabula rasa* is symptomatic for the spirit of revolt pointed at the past and afflicting the present time. It was the impatience that sometimes created the radical liberals from the protagonists of the "theory of optimal planning and functioning of the socialist economy" over night. In other few cases, the *fundamentalist neo-classical economists* represented by Václav Klaus and his followers have rejected to provide any reasons for the adaptation of economic theory to the completely different institutional frameworks of real socialism and transforming economy, respectively.

The main goal of the Czech privatization became the speed of the change – speed at all costs. The idol of instrumental rationality, the conviction that exclusively intentional causality and consequentionalism motivate economic behavior, all this shaped the strategy of privatization. The moral grounds of the market economy have been omitted. But the concrete form of the emerging order of market cannot be evolved without an agency of history and belief structures of market participants leading the processes of learning by doing (Heap, Sh. H. 1989). A reconstruction of the institutional framework of economy does not mean the ideologically formulated postulates of private property, but the education of new owners to the faith in order and its rules, the civic virtues, learning business ethics by doing.

3. The Speedy Privatization
without Firm Rules Endangers the Order

A general question of modern economies is the right division of labor between markets and hierarchies (Williamson, O. E. 1977). Real socialism developed a very specific and very ineffective solution to this problem. The sudden dissolution of the planning system and governing hierarchical structures have disordered the unsatisfying but existing balance of the vertical and horizontal co-ordination of the system. As a general result, two quantitatively well measurable phenomena have appeared: steep increase in mutual indebtedness of enterprises, and steep increase in the number of law cases at commerce courts (hundreds of thousands of court presentations a year).

The principle of enforcement of property rights has become almost totally ineffective. Andrei Schleifer has shown that the insufficiency of legal enforcement gives rise to public demand for the creation of private mechanisms for property rights protection and for the recovery of claims, leading to a very undesirable side phenomena that is dangerous to society: private arbitration of disputes connected with *violence* and Mafia tricks usual in *organized crime*. (Schleifer, A. 1994)

The intrinsic logic of the overall process has unavoidably resulted in a state in which the criterion of the speed of privatization has become counterproductive: the faster was a progress in divisibility of property rights, the steeper was the drop in their enforcement at least in the legal one. The price-liberalization and the fast disassembling of planning hierarchy opened the door for the dynamic forces of market co-ordination and this is – comparatively to the "shortage economy" – a positive trend to the market order. But also a process of transition has to be subjected to some order. According to Hayek, the order is a state of society that enables people to form the right expectations based on social regularities. (Hayek, F. A. von 1982) Relating to this concept of order, I have to insist on the very controversial course of the Czech fast transformation, the counter-productivity of speed.

Institutional economics has discovered that the fundament for the contractual and financial discipline is private ordering as the result of the very long evolution of stabilized market economies. Lacking private ordering leads inevitably to the illusive reliance on "legal centralism" and the state as guarantor of justice in the economy fails in one of its key functions. The business courts are, for a few years, blocked by the piles of untransacted presentations and unsolved contract conflicts. The institution of bankruptcy procedure is too slow, too ineffective and too expensive.

During the period of so-called *pre-privatization agony* (a term from the vocabulary of the Czech government economists used for the state of things "neither plan – nor market") the government completely resigned on the control of "corporate governance." State enterprises have been fully controlled by managers and in the system of liberalized prices and free entrepreneurship (open also for the top managers of state enterprises), the clear definition of the act, known as "theft" in legal systems, practically disappeared. The door has been broadly open to non-transparent transfers of assets from state to private hands.

A completely new Czech term *"tunneling"* appeared, including the whole set of patterns of behavior in "striping assets," some of them of the typical "Czech inventions and innovations at the improper field," product of learning by doing during four decades of "real socialism" where the new proverb prevailed: "everybody who does not steal is stealing his own family!" After all, theft is usually the fastest way of property rights transactions, and pure instrumental rationality eventually doesn't have to object to anything. (As to the more detailed description of the patterns of striping assets in the Czech republic I refer to my earlier paper presented in 1994 in Rome. (Mlčoch, L. 1994))

The theorem of Ronald Coase has been used and abused as the theoretical justification of the ideology that tolerates the ways and methods of "wild privatization." In the imaginary world with zero transaction costs, the original distribution of wealth does not matter.

Reading carefully the Nobel lecture of Ronald Coase that was prepared in 1991 when the transformation of property right structures was in progress in post-communist countries, one would clearly recognize that the laureate is challenging to the study of societies with non-zero transaction costs and not to the application of his theorem, which is valid for the ideal world only, but to the real world in which the basic assumptions of ideals are missing. And the transaction costs in modern societies are too important (if not even prohibitive) to take no account of. For example, the institutional investors in emerging Czech capital markets have shown patterns of behavior escaping from "textbooks." Insider trading, distorted information, manipulated or completely lacking reporting, opportunistic behavior and moral hazard are used to the expropriation of their own small shareholders. I refer to my more detailed description in this connection (Mlčoch, L. 1995).

Unfortunately, until now, there is not sufficient political will to establish standard institutions for the regulation of the Czech capital market. This example is also instructive to support my hypothesis about trade off between the speed of change and business ethics.

The concentration of property is seen from the instrumental rationality point of view as an inevitable process. The small shareholders don't have yet sufficient legal safeguards against the discrimination from the side of "core investors" and also their own institutions. The reasons for the postponement of legal protection are clear: this protection could cause slow-down in the process of property rights concentration. So, for the strategy of radical and misunderstood liberalism some business ethics or "social justice" considerations have to be put aside. There is also the alternative explanation of this lacking political will, i.e. the invested interests of pirates on capital markets who prefer the jungle and block the establishing of firm rules.

Besides the endangering of legal and economic order from the side of "wild privatization" tolerated with tacit consensus "from above," there is also a certain trade off between the speed of privatization "from below" and order. The responsible entrepreneurship is closely connected with the institution of liability. In our Czech conditions, only the amount of 100.000 Czech crowns ($\approx$ 5.000 DM) is sufficient to the foundation of private company limited by guarantee and for the shareholder company (Ltd.) only 1 million crowns ($\approx$ 50.000 DM) is necessary. The number of newly founded small businesses "on green field" is impressive. Nevertheless, as soon as the volume of transactions exceeds the invested capital about several orders of magnitude, the liability is nothing else than a fiction. The *freedom* in private economic activities is *not balanced* with *responsibility*, and the door is open even for completely speculative and fraudulent practices shifting the economy into a criminal world.

By the way, the situation of lacking capital for the foundation of new companies was typical just for the "investment privatization funds", the *spiritus movens* of the Czech voucher scheme. The stewardship of giant institutions has no backing in the liability. The negligible liability of institutions is the main reason for their deep dependence on banks.

So, the evolution of private ownership under the characterized strategy of radical liberalism acquires certain specific ethical and cultural features that endanger the emerging order and the stability of society. The Czech economy is shifted on the imaginary map of Europe to the "south-east direction."

4. Fast Privatization at the State Expenses is Endangered by Formalism

Lacking domestic capital has had influence also on the chosen methods of privatization. Even during the distribution of public capital assets "free of charge," the case of Czech Republic has shown that the restructuring of property esp. in the concentrated institutional form of "institutions," leads to a conservation of some essential dysfunctions of the past system. In particular, it does not provide any effective solution of the core problem of the operationalization of property rights, i.e. the problem of corporate governance. David Stark applies the term "recombined property" for Hungarian transformation. (Stark, D. 1996) Nevertheless, his argumentation is easily transferable to the Czech conditions.

Referring to my earlier studies on the behavior of the enterprise sphere in real socialism, and having investigated the "Czech hybrid" resulted from the voucher scheme; Peter Kenya has come to the same conclusion. (Kenya, P. 1994)

As if the principle of path dependency shows that the weight of "institutional memory" of four decades of real socialism is more important than the differences in privatization strategies of particular countries that have lasted only for several years. So, the "recombinant property" is present also in the Czech Republic. The state has formally withdrawn from the economy (Fund of National Property administers only about 20% of national property), making believe that the privatization process is almost finished.

However, the role of state is far more important than it may appear at the first look. The non-functional hierarchical structure has been revitalized. The state still remains the core investor in the major financial institutions that founded the largest privatization investment funds. These funds manage portfolios that involve two hundred to five hundred companies (often more property than was administered by the former resort ministries). The state is still an indirect shareholder of the property in an important sector of the economy (private from the formal legal point of view), and it can be designated as the "core investor" (in terms of the theory of corporate governance).

Consequently, the state cannot avoid its proprietor responsibility. The state has remained as the greatest creditor of many large and medium size enterprises, due to the old liabilities transferred to the state financial institution, called "Konsolidační banka" (Consolidation Bank), but also through non-paid taxes, social and health insurance, etc. Even high numbers of enterprises that were formally privatized by means of direct sale or public tender belong to this category because of their inability to pay off their debts to the Fund of National Property. (The scandalous case of Poldi Steel Kladno is only a top of iceberg.)

Many companies are thus private in name only. Unsolved problem of agency, the non-competitive financial structures caused that even the term "banking socialism" appeared, the unintended product of the "short" Czech way of privatization. Pavel Mertlík, deputy Prime Minister for economy in the social democratic party government, called the Czech privatization ironically as the way from public ownership to public ownership. (Mertlik, P. 1995) I prefer the term "quasi-private ownership."

If this skepticism would prevail, the argument of Iván Szelényi from University of California at Los Angeles is compelling: "it may not be possible to convert public ownership into genuinely individual private property. Even the 'most primitive' (and most brutal) accumulation of capital may not be fast enough to generate the wealth which would be necessary for individual private ownership in the corporate sector of the economy." (Szelényi, I. 1995, p. 9.)

5. Privatization: The Conflict between Efficiency and Social Justice?

P. H. Dembinski has presented the principal criticism of the functioning of international capital markets. The property represented by prevailing ephemeral capital transactions with speculative motivations is the hidden and incomplete property. The reduction of property rights only to *usus fructus* and *abusus* resulted in the state, that *usus* – the primary function of property rights, the implication of which is the ownership responsibility, is almost completely lacking. (Dembinski, P. H. 1995)

The formal private property evolving from the fast mass privatization suffers by the illness of partial functioning of property rights to a much greater extent. During "real socialism," quasi-ownership forms flourished, based on "positional property," "party nomenclature entitlements" or the property *de facto*. For the real socialism elite the only function of property rights has been substantial: i.e. *usus fructus*. The responsibility for the negative results of "entrepreneurship" has been completely socialized and legal transactions with property rights not allowed (i.e. both *usus* and *abusus* were lacking).

Now, as a result of the fast and mass privatization in the situation of lacking domestic capital, in the sector of formally privatized economy we are discussing, the negative results of business are still socialized to a great extent. Legal transactions with property rights are without a doubt permitted but strictly restricted by high transaction costs and insufficient financial liquidity. The exceptional chance to create the immense concentration of economic power and wealth turned up for those groups that benefited from the redistribution consequences of opportunities for insider trading and adjoining to "recombined property right structures." And these favored "investors" enjoy predominantly the fruits of (quasi)private property (*usus fructus*) whilst there are no responsible owners we are still waiting for.

Piotr Jasinski and George Yarrow object to the "long way" of privatization (more precisely to its extreme form represented exclusively by the privatization "from below"), that this way should lead to the creation of a "dual economy," unresolved agency problems, and the financial burdens imposed by public sector on the rest of the economy, i.e. on the private sector evolving "from below." (Jasinski, P. & Yarrow, G. 1995) Well, then all these phenomena of the dual economy are manifesting their presence within the Czech formally privatized economy along the "short way." The quasi-private state banks continue in the execution of the former functions of socialist planning and managing hierarchy, i.e. financial redistribution and paternalistic protection, the guarantee of economic survival. The policy uses different tools (esp. credit and interest conditions, liquidation of debts from the state resources). The postponed restructuring, low rate of unemployment and passive foreign trade balance are the main consequences of accepted strategy of privatization.

This rather sceptic view of the efficiency outcome of the Czech fast privatization lead me of course to the next question which is the problem of social justice and "fair play." Jasinski and Yarrow formulated the so called "non-expropriation criterion": the effort to prevent social injustice in privatization favored the partial interests of privileged groups esp. old structures of party nomenclature. They pronounced a hypothesis, that the efficiency argument of fast distribution of property rights free of charge could justify even the expropriation of shares on public property not fully consistent with social justice and fairness. But, if my critical view on efficiency outcome of voucher scheme is correct, then the last reasons for justification of the social injustices coming from consequences of property right redistribution disappear. I confess that every trade off between the ethics (and fairness) and efficiency subjected to some thinking over is rather suspicious for me. And it seems to be sure that we touch in this connection the deepest reasons for the lost social consensus in the economic transformation in the Czech republic.

The strongest reason for privatization explains in fact the hypothesis of "interest groups" in a modern theory of property rights. "The ability to influence elected representatives is often strong in the case of relatively small, compact special-interest groups, where each individual has much to gain by an adjustment in the structure of property rights." (Eggertsson, Th. 1992, p. 276) The massive and fast privatization is the best empirical test of this theory. Therefore, the rent-seeking and wealth-seeking behavior of members from control groups in the enterprises and from the "old structures" of the governance hierarchy – the exclusiveness of their positions was exceptional – provides an explanation of the decisive moving forces for the speed of change. Eagerness and covetousness are perhaps the deepest propensities to privatize without firm rules and as fast as possible.

But what we urgently need now in our country is a deep social, political and certainly spiritual conversion as well: the understanding that the liberal doctrine is fatally connected with the concept of common good, that private initiative and freedom have to be well balanced with firm and enforceable rules for which the guarantor is a sufficiently strong state, and finally that the market economy does not work without a moral foundation. All these three pillars of liberalism are certainly valid not only in the Czech Republic but also everywhere in the world and they focus our attention on the principal topics, the *Ethics of Capitalism*.

6. Czech Style Capitalism

It seems that in the years since the fall of communism in 1989, a specific Czech type of capitalism has been born. It's almost like a special type of "state capitalism" or "mixed economy" which has assumed many of the dysfunctional characteristics of the previous period of "real socialism." Some have described it as an "excessively soft capitalism," while others have seen it as a Kafkaesque route that led from public ownership back to public ownership. Critics with a more conservative orientation have started to doubt whether the current Czech system has anything at all to do with capitalism and have started to use the term "banking socialism" to describe it.

The brunt of the criticism has been reserved for the sector of so-called "recombined ownership," a term devised by David Stark to denote ownership which may be formally private but is actually a continuation of a more or less hidden state paternalism. Jan Sokol, as I have mentioned earlier, referred to certain aspects of Czech capitalism as "gangster liberalism." Others have an even simpler explanation for the state of the Czech economy: despite former prime minister Václav Klaus's rhetoric and constant warnings about the dangers of adopting a "free market with adjectives," we simply haven't even managed to establish "standard capitalism" in our country.

I do not want to make light of the need for fundamental systemic changes during the process of abandoning the institutions of "real socialism." The transformation of a socialist economy and society is a problem with several dimensions. Society must be a modernized and restructured society and the rule of law must be cultivated. Society also needs a dimension of visions, dreams, hopes, and ideals. After 1989, Czech society faced the task of a complete cultural overhaul. The idea that the economy was the most important dimension has foundered. The mistake was based on an instrumentalist interpretation of institutions.

It was the fathers of social market economics in the post-war Germany who worked their way to the conclusion that the economy must be based on meta-economic values and that it should not focus solely on economic efficiency. Wilhelm Röpke pointed out that only once the system respects human dignity it could expect greater material productivity. The Czech transformation, which established privatization as the road to rationalization and efficiency and sacrificed ethical questions in order to set those goals as its overriding purpose, was simply doomed to fail – even as far as its own goal of economic prosperity was concerned.

Who will be the bearer of the ethos in our specific Czech conditions? Does morality require a transcendental source or will our society be satisfied with a secular humanism? Is the highly secular Czech society open to a new evangelization? Do we need a truly Catholic social ethic to revive the spirit of capitalism, as that renowned American academic Michael Nowak believes? Should we be put our faith in the synod of the Czech Catholic Church, which will be launched at the very end of this millennium? And if it is not realistic to expect some kind of a turnaround in this regard, where will we then find the strength and will to cultivate our political and economic behavior? I don't know the answers to these questions.

Many people in the Czech Republic seem firmly convinced that there are no options when it comes to transforming the economy. For instance, Klaus' espousal of "capitalism without adjectives" was textbook dogmatism as if there were no other reasonable alternative. It is revealing to note that the same mistake is being repeated today. The idea that the next government, no matter who will be in it, will have "zero room to maneuver" has suddenly gained currency in this country. This is an especially fascinating aspect of the Czech political scene. First, we had the unreformable concept of real socialism to which no alternatives were permitted and therefore there was "zero room to maneuver." Following the collapse of real socialism, a unique Czech vision of radical liberal transformation appeared – and once again we were told that there were no permissible alternatives. Today, we have, yet again, "zero room to maneuver" if we want to forge ahead with the transformation process.

I fear that such formulations hide a shaken identity and personal integrity as well as a lack of faith. Historical determinism may be the philosophy of slaves, but human beings were born free.

After the failure of real socialism, two different interpretations were offered as explanations of the new situation. According to American analyst Francis Fukuyama, we were witnessing the end of history in the form of the sweeping victory of political and economic liberalism within one global system. According to French analyst Michel Albert, we were entering a new stage of competition between various models of capitalism. A few years later, Albert's theory has been scarred several times and we are certainly not approaching the end of history. Today, one might characterize international developments as the continuing globalization of the world economy and the enduring differentiation of both formal and informal cultural institutions.

Our sweet, little country in the middle of Europe is part of these worldwide developments. The trick is to plug into the global economy without losing our integrity and individuality. At the moment, we don't have much of one or the other. Or, to put it more precisely, we don't have much of the former because we surrendered the latter. We didn't have a convincing vision, enough faith in a strong, and ourselves enough political and civic will to remain true to ourselves after 1989. Little wonder, when one thinks of how many historical upheavals we Czechs have gone through during this century. Several times, we have been caught in the wheelworks of history and several times our ownership relations have been disrupted and destabilized. Our morals have also gone through several upheavals and many years of erosion.

We lived through the conclusion of the Habsburg monarchy with the alliance of the "throne and the altar" and the morals of Catholicism, perhaps a little hypocritical and a little worn out – which all vanished in the slaughterhouse of World War I. Then came the 20 interwar years of Czechoslovakia's First Republic, with its de-Austrianization and "down with Rome" slogans and its attempts to bring us a little closer to the capitalism of the Anglo-Saxon world. Next came World War II and the years we spent as a protectorate of Nazi Germany and its wartime economy, this was when the idea that the state didn't belong to us first took root and thievery and sloth started to smack of patriotism. The first three post-war years were marked by the "mixed economy" theory, ethnic cleansing aimed at the Sudeten Germans, and the expropriation of property and its "national management." Then came the communist era and the Soviet model which was partially forced on us and which we partially adopted with enthusiasm. It was based on the mass nationalization of property en bloc without compensation, in other words, mass and organized robbery.

Years went by during which a certain economic morality surfaced around the slogan, "Anyone who doesn't steal from the state is stealing from his or her own family." Then came the collapse of real socialism and the period of "pre-privatization agony," during which the term "theft" lost all meaning. Finally, we witnessed the so-called "tunneling" of banks, companies, and investment funds – a brand new term that the Czech Republic gave to the world.

The rhetoric of radical liberalism, which dominated the political discourse in this country during the first half of the 1990s, often seemed almost messianic and apocalyptic in its scope and irrationalism. Some Czech historians say that such furious bursts of activity – when Czechs start to feel like they are the center of the world – are typical of the modern history of this nation. They are generally followed by long periods of skepticism. It seems that we are now entering one of those pessimistic phases and that the public is no longer inclined toward any grand visions or promises. Perhaps it might even be inclined to accept a modest political program involving a series of small steps that would eventually lead to some for of orderly state. We need to return to the "long way," which asides form other things means the acceptance of certain proven institutional elements from the past. In my opinion, one of these elements is the relatively significant and irreplaceable role of the state and the institution of corporativism in the civic, professional, and interest group spheres.

In a geographic or geopolitical sense, there are great paradoxes in the recent orientation of "Czech capitalism" of the 1990s. Forty years of real socialism shunted us off to the eastern side of that imaginary map of European social values, toward some kind of Orwellian Eurasia. After 1989, the unrealistic attempts to apply the ideas of the Chicago school of economic theory in our region did not lead to the establishment of the Anglo-Saxon model of capitalism in the Czech Republic. On the contrary, it shunted us off in a southeastern direction, toward the Balkans. Some analysts have traced similarities between the emerging Central and Eastern European economies and those of the Latin American countries. Those countries are marked by dysfunctional parliamentary democracies, ill-defined divisions between the private and public sectors, corruption, and the encroachment of the criminal economy into state institutions. And this points to the greatest paradox of all the Czech transformation process. There is pronounced distaste in this country for the Western European model of capitalism, which by all accounts should seem closer to us due to our historical and cultural ties to that region. Isn't it time to return home from our wanderings? Isn't it time to come back to the good old Central Europe?

In sharp dichotomy to the former government's liberal rhetoric stand the obvious results of the Czech transformation so far. We now have a "dual economy" where companies that have "recombined ownership" – that is, they are still under the influence of a relatively intense state paternalism – far exceeds the 20% of companies which the government claims "remain to be privatized." Many formally private companies in which the state has a more or less hidden share have continued to rely on the state to keep them afloat as they pay out wages and distribute profits while losing money due to financial mismanagement or worse (although it is always hard to prove criminal intention in such cases). It is a type of perverse behavior which already existed under real socialism and which is known in the Anglo-Saxon world as "rent- and wealth-seeking behavior." The social costs of these "privatization games" are borne above all by the profits gained from the privatization of property that has truly been privatized. Whatever the banks cannot cover by raising interest rates on loans to healthy companies which are making real profits is covered by the state budget and thus by the taxpayers, which are the last instance in the financial coverage of the "recombined ownership" concept.

Many observers believe that the solution to these problems, which are now more or less accepted as such, lies in the quick privatization of the rest of the economy. I am convinced that this is once again the wrong recipe. The conversion of "recombined ownership" forms into standard ownership forms is necessary, but I don't believe it is realistic to expect that complete privatization can be achieved within a short period of time. You need two sides for privatization to occur: the buyer and the seller. If a piece of privatized property has a null or even negative market value, the state has to be willing to cough up money in order to get rid of it. Such transfers of property carry an asymmetric risk. The private buyer of the property is essentially risking nothing at all while the state – especially when it comes to the large, strategic companies and banks – is taking a moral gamble and remains a hostage of private capital because, for political reasons, no government can allow such companies to go bankrupt and thereby threaten the stability of entire regions and sectors.

The "recombined ownership" schemes should be dismantled in a process that includes two contradictory strategies – real privatization wherever possible or the resumption of state control over companies wherever the re-nationalization of poorly privatized firms is a lesser evil than mass regional unemployment regions and the loss of money still owed to the state. The strange form of etatism that has been practiced in this country until now should be replaced with an open and transparent policy of privatization. However, nationalization in those sectors for which there is no reasonable alternative must take place only exceptionally and in full accordance with the law – which means that the current owners should receive compensation. The ideological hysteria, which was recently stirred up in the Czech media when I suggested this plan at a ongress of the Christian Democratic Union-Czech People's Party, simply demonstrates how indoctrinated and ideological this society has become.

But these are all temporary problems. As to the long-term prospects of the Czech Republic, I am an optimist. I am convinced that during the first decade of the new millennium, "Czech capitalism" will continue to be based on the principles of a "mixed economy" in which the state will play an essential role. It will be a state that is aware of its ownership responsibilities and thus its role in the restructuring of companies in the industrial sector. It will also be a state that is more professional, more distinct from the private sphere, and more able to fulfill its role as a guarantor of the legal will system. The proper role of the business ethics of capitalism will be understood even in the Czech Republic. I believe that our Czech society will eventually come to accept that *morality* is not a luxury but a *source* of the *wealth* of *nations*.

Humanizing the Economy: On the Relationship between the Ethics of Human Rights and Economic Discourse

Stefano Zamagni
University of Bologna
Italy

1. Introduction and Motivation

We live in a time in which a growing number of social scientists and philosophers-theologians are discussing, with growing frequency, themes of common interest, advancing new avenues of research and proposing new grounds for debate. This renewed interest comes after several decades during which the two scientific areas, once quite close to each other, developed in substantial isolation from each other. It cannot be denied that for many scholars this separation remains unbridged.

Many philosophers-theologians, on one side, and social scientists, on the other side, still maintain that to take under serious consideration the categories of thought employed in the other discipline is either lowering their professional status or, at best, irrelevant. On the other hand, it is a fact that today more and more scholars, among those who show an interest in probing the temper of their research, find it useful and inspiring to try to overcome that separation.

It is precisely within such a framework – which resembles a sort of intellectual migration – that the question of the relationship between the ethics of human rights (EHR) and economics as a scientific discourse can be dealt with. Indeed, what kind of relationship is there between EHR and economics? Which problems arise by way of closer collaboration between them? Ignoring the multiplicity of individual answers, these can be grouped in two main sets. On the one hand, there are those who claim that EHR should act as a matrix within which economics takes shape as scientific discourse and draws strength for its theories. On the other hand, there is the position of those – nowadays the majority – who believe that all EHR can, and hence ought to offer the economist, is a twofold support: to suggest selection criteria for prioritizing economic problems; or to provide guidelines for the practical utilization of the results obtained by the economist. However, during the process of production of economic knowledge the horizon offered by EHR is next to irrelevant, indeed it is jealously kept apart. An example may help to clarify the point: EHR may suggest that searching into the unemployment question should be a priority in the economist's agenda; or it may advise on how to distribute fairly among its citizens the income produced in a country. How one arrives at a specific theory of the labor market or how one is capable of explaining the level of income produced by a certain economy is totally unconcerned with the value options stemming from EHR.

It seems to me that both positions are aporetic and therefore unacceptable, if on different grounds. The first one, because it would disclaim the autonomy of economic science. As within economics the well-known avalutativity thesis – according to which science has to be value-neutral – was asserting itself, a trend was gaining ground to consider knowledge produced by economic thinking as devoid of any practical leading function. Economic science – the argument goes – does not accompany nor does it guide decision-makers' actions, whatever they may be, but rather, it sees and foresees human actions just as the physicist anticipates nature's motions. The acceptance of the avalutativity character as borderline to scientific learning, once combined with the concept that only the latter can be considered as rigorously rational, led to assume avalutativity as a feature essentially inherent in economic reasoning. This is equivalent to saying that for an economist to be a scientist he cannot commit himself to judgments of value. Ends and dispositions are declared irrelevant to scientific reason, which has nothing to say about them; hence the spreading of relativistic – not to say skeptical – attitudes among economists, even among those who declare themselves believers.

The uneasy position produced by this lack of orientation is obvious to many modern scholars. This is especially true of those economists who are wont to question the scientific status of their own discipline, as is not unusual today. If we construe economics as one – certainly not the only one – way to improve our understanding of the social world and to help to improve certain social structures (for example, the welfare system), the economist cannot self-limit his/her action range to efficiency issues. Above all, he/she cannot pretend to ignore that the wider the magnitude of decisions to be made, the more urgent the need to clarify the criteria which underlie decision-making. "Even though he is aware of all this – writes Jonas – the economic specialist still feels compelled to deny his science the status to supply those selection criteria, hence the authority to say "yes" or "no" to any proposed objective with the obvious exception of decisions merely concerning feasibility. Furthermore, if asked whether economic knowledge should be judge or a mere performer of its ends, the purist replies by choosing the latter. Such is the reply of scientific asceticism that he/she abides by in the name of economics' scientific purity." (Jonas, J. 1991, p. 142.) Yet we know today that values and scientific enquiry do not necessarily have to clash, as Pascal in modern times bravely maintained.

The extent to which this "scientific asceticism" is harming the comprehension of the problems of a post-industrial society and how far it contributed to making EHR a sort of pure ethical code of conduct is manifest to all. To me, EHR's proper contribution to a transdisciplinary methodology in the realm of social science is to be found in the offering of a hermeneutical horizon promoting a change of those categories of thought that are the basis of economic discourse.

Needless to say, any attempt to restore within economic discourse the perspective of EHR is sure to be well received, at least not opposed, by the profession, more specifically by avowed non-believers, provided one can prove that such retrieval, while taking place in full compliance with the canons of scientific practice, will be of help in correcting some aporias and filling gaps in the discipline. In other words, one needs to be able to prove that the introduction of EHR categories into the developing process of economic thinking can widen, not restrict, the cognitive range of economic science, thus enabling it to firm up its grip on reality. My point, then, is that the most significant contribution that such an attempt can nowadays offer for a reconceptualization of economic discourse lies in its capability to answer the following question: is it possible to humanize the economy and, if so, how can this be achieved? Given the present historical circumstance in which the only existing economic model is the market economy – neither command economy nor the celebrated mixed economy representing any longer credible alternatives – the question could also be rendered as follows: is it possible to humanize the market, that is, is it possible to figure out a model of market capable of tentatively including *all* human beings and of estimating *all* of the human person in his/her multifaceted dimensions?

The pages that follow, presenting a twofold argument, should be read against this background. The first one is to provide a criticism – however concise – of that unique thought that is the "one best way." It should be noted that this kind of criticism is all the more necessary if we bear in mind the tendency, which we observe in reality, to derive a "unique policy" from that unique thought. The second task is to produce arguments supporting the thesis that it is possible to generate a consensus about the proposal of civil economy as a viable path towards humanizing the market. The format I am adopting here aims at warding off the risk of remaining, on one side, above reality through utopia, and on the other side, beneath reality through resignation.

2. On the Unique Thought of the "Best Way"

The unique thought of the now so fashionable "one best way" suggests with unrelenting persistence, and thus leads us to believe, the following representation of our market society. (Zamagni, S. 1999a) The market is a contextualized institution resting on a clearly defined structure of accepted norms. It is obvious that legal norms cannot completely steer economic decisions, nor do they alone suffice to regulate entirely economic interaction. Within the existing framework of norms, culture and competition – "the two determining agencies in market economies," to use J. S. Mill's words, (Schlicht, E. 1998, p. 23.) – will then answer the call. The specific significance of these two agencies is clearly not the same in the various historical phases: in traditional societies (pre-capitalistic ones) culture, viewed here as a body of social norms and conventions, is the driving agency; in modern societies instead the drive of competition prevails insofar as such forces progressively erode those spaces of economic activity which rest upon social norms and conventions. An implication of such a vision is that in time the sphere of economic relations is going to be almost totally ruled by the forces of competition alone, which is tantamount to saying that the modern age viewed as a phase in the cultural evolution process inexorably tends to replace interpersonal relations with anonymous and impersonal market laws.

Of course, even advocates of the "one best way" have to admit that such a substitution will never be a total one. "Culture" can at no time be completely replaced by "competition" for the obvious reason that there shall always be spaces of economic activity in which the ruling principle of the exchange of equivalents is not going to apply. As we well know, this is the principle ruling familiar market transaction as they are described in economic textbooks. Even the most modern market society will include a sphere of economic relations, which, whether or not they transit through the market, will be governed by social conventions and rules. This is the sphere of activities making up the nonprofit or third sector. It should be observed however that this has to remain a residual sphere of relations with limited quantitative impact and in any case such that it should in no way impair the operational logic of competition: precisely, a third sector. So much so that serious problems arise as soon as non-profit activities exceed a determined dimension, thus leaving the niche within which they could enjoy full legitimacy. With regard to this, the situation of the USA is illuminating. In that country a subtle reaction has been going on for some years, aimed at delegitimizing non-profit organizations. At the moment this action is pursued chiefly at the academic-scientific level (there are several working papers allegedly evidencing that the management by non-profit organizations of hospitals or welfare institutions is socially inefficient). One first sign at political level has, however, already been perceived: the Istook Amendment at the 104th USA Congress in November 1998 suggested the cancellation of all fiscal benefits accruing to some specific non profit organizations. (The bill presented by Republican Senator Istook eventually failed to pass by a few votes). (Salamon, L. 1999)

This dichotomous portrayal of the reality of market societies generates a twofold disastrous consequence. From the viewpoint of the division of labor among disciplines, in the course of the last century the separation has been crystallizing between economics as the science which deals only with the sphere of economic facts and has *homo œconomicus* as its specific mode of explanation, and sociology as the science dealing only with social facts, with *homo sociologicus* as its explanatory paradigm. The result thereof is that these disciplines, which should and could be complementary, ended up by each acquiring a specific identity precisely due to the assumption of such division.

The second, assuredly more significant consequence has been the emergence of a line of thinking which identifies the market as the idealtypical place in which subjects are prompted to act *only* out of self-interest, whatever the latter may be – whether selfish or apparently un-selfish. Indeed, in the wake of the theory of Gary Becker, cofounder of the Chicago School and Nobel Prize laureate for economics, altruism is nothing but disguised selfishness or at best enlightened egoism – exactly as in Nietzsche's lapidary and cynical statement "your neighbour praises the absence of selfishness because he benefits from it." Thus the conviction has been gaining strength that the only judgment of value the market can sustain is that of efficiency, conceived as the appraisal of the adequacy of means in view of the maximum (possible) achievement of the interests of the participants in the market game. It is easy to explain why this could happen. If the only motivation leading individuals to operate in the market is the pursuit of self-interest, it is obvious that the only possible assessment of market outcomes is whether or not the latter are the best in relation to the initially available resources. To entrust the market process with other ends, for example economic justice, is un-thinkable. The market cannot, hence should not, be charged with such ends.

As the supporters themselves of this line of thinking admit, there are other values that the market as institution has to take into account, but they stand, so-to-say, at the beginning and relate to the basic conditions for the market to come into being and regularly operate. Think of values such as freedom, honesty and trust. One does, indeed, recognize that these values are necessary for an efficient market performance: in fact, it would not even exist without freedom of enterprise or without free-dom to enter exchange relations. Likewise, if economic agents do not meet their obligations, do not comply with the law in force, and, above all, if no close-knit network of trust relations is established, the market cannot possibly operate. However, according to mainstream, economic thinking all of this should be in existence before market operations be-gin. In any case, it is not the market's task to provide it; it is, rather, the task of the civil society and /or of the State.

Needless to say, the unique thought of the "one best way" is not even touched on by the doubt that results produced by the market process might eventually erode that core of values upon which it rests and with-out which any market economy would be extremely short-lived. If, for example, market outcomes do not comply with some standard of distributive justice, how can one assume that the values of honesty and trust will continue to support the market itself? St. Augustine provides a cogent answer of extraordinary freshness when he writes "What is a community of citizens other than a multitude of people bound to one another by the tie of concord? In the State, what musicians call harmony is concord: civic concord cannot exist without justice" (*Civ. Dei*, 2, 21). Indeed, why should economic agents trust one another and meet their obligations if there is a perception or even full awareness that the outcome of the market process is plainly unjust?

The line of thought I am here sketching obviously cannot wholly disclaim the significance of questions like the ones I have been raising and which could be re-formulated as follows: what becomes of the interests or fate of those who, for one reason or another, fail to participate in the market game or are turned out of it as losers or because they lagged too far behind the winners? The answer, which is provided, is the State, an institution, which is legitimized to intervene directly in the economic sphere, each time this is necessary in order to cancel or to compensate socially disastrous consequences associated to the market functioning. In this way, however, the gap between the sphere of efficiency judgments and the sphere of value judgments widens instead of narrowing. In the first place, because this vision strengthens the belief that market is an allocative mechanism which can function *in vacuo*, regardless of the kind of society in which it is embedded, which means that the market is visualized as an ethically neutral mechanism whose results can be corrected by the State whenever they appear unacceptable by some standard of justice. In the second place, because it substantiates the idea that the market area coincides with the one in which only individual interests are protected, and the State area as the one in which collective interests are protected. Hence the well-known dichotomous social order that identifies the State as the forum of public interests (i.e., of solidarity) and the market as the forum of privatism (that is, as the arena in which only individual purposes are pursued). It is the "public," *viz.* the State that has to take care of solidarity by means of redistribution (the "rich" are taxed and the receipts are redistributed to the "poor"). The "private," i.e. the market, should take care of efficiency, *viz.* of the optimal production of wealth and of philanthropy or "charity" at the most.

3. The Undefendable Thesis of the "Best Way"

What does not stand scrutiny in the description of market societies as outlined above, a description apparently so convincing and widespread in popular culture as to make it seem impregnable, almost a truth to be received without criticism?

In the first place, such a representation is misleading because law, culture and competition are not alternative instruments to solve the problems of social order, more specifically those connected with the coordination of economic decisions. These instruments are instead complementary, for the basic reason that, if market transactions rely upon social and legal norms prevailing at a given time, it is likewise true that the economic process itself tends to modify such norms. In other words, there is a substantial *co-evolution* between norms and economic behaviors. Therefore, the distinction between the paradigms of *homo œconomicus* and of *homo sociologicus* is after all not so reliable as we were always made to believe. In fact, it is true that the more recent theory of evolutionary games has attempted to explain the outcomes of (social and legal) norms by viewing them as *routines* that are adopted since they appear as the winners, in competitive terms, in the solution of both coordination and bargaining problems. Along this line, such theory has pretended to demonstrate that any social relation can be examined essentially as an exchange relation, and therefore the problem of a social theory would simply reduce to a problem of exchange. It follows that what at a first glance may seem to be a *rule-following* behavior, turns out to be a typical problem of rational choice in only slightly more complex contexts, which is tantamount to saying that every *homo sociologicus* ultimately harbors an ever-busy homunculus *œconomicus*.

This instrumentalist conception of social and legal norms is unacceptable on two different grounds. On the one hand, it may account at most for coordination problems such as "why one travels on the right hand side of the street," but fails to explain why even in total absence of sanctions some people will conform to very demanding rules, or why there are people who donate anonymously or offer very active service on a purely volunteer basis, and so forth. On the other hand, because the instrumentalist conception of norms may be fine as long as we investigate *how* one chooses, but when it comes to explaining *why* one does, it is impossible to assume that values are just a datum of the problem. As adroitly pointed out by Becattini, in economic discourse there seems to be a predominance of studies assuming that "some of the most intrinsically human peculiarities of the economic agent such as his notions of justice, honour, loyalty and also his vaguest hopes and illusions [are] pre-economic data, or 'accidental deviations from the rational norm' which reciprocally compensate within the vast body of data." (Becattini, G. 1999)

Secondly, it is not true that maximum extension of the market area improves everybody's well-being. The aphorism according to which "a rising tide raises all boats" is not true. As we know, this is the most favorite metaphor with the recent liberal-individualistic formulation according to which, the well-being of people being a function of economic prosperity which in turn is linked to the spread of market relations, the actual priority of political action should be an effort to ensure all those conditions (fiscal, public administration, optimum allocation of property rights and so on) which foster a flourishing of markets. In that vision, the welfare state that redistributes, via taxation, wealth while keeping itself outside the wealth-producing mechanism, hampers economic growth, all the more so when it is greedy (causing major distorting effects in the market) and when its instruments are submitted to political uses, thus jeopardizing normal democratic dialectics. Hence the recommendation that the welfare system should take care solely of those whom the market contest leaves on the fringes of society. The others, those who manage to stay inside the virtuous circle of economic growth, will take care of their own protection by availing themselves of the numerous solutions offered by private insurance schemes.

Where is the weak point in such argument? It is to be found in the simple reason that the prerequisite of equal opportunities for all is one that must apply throughout the life-span of citizens and not just *una tantum*, the moment they enter the economic arena. To put it another way, for all participants to enjoy actual conditions of freedom it is not sufficient to ensure equal opportunities at the start of the economic race. The market contest is indeed quite different from a sports contest. In the latter, the most gifted or capable wins the prize but this in no way confers upon him the possibility of, or bestows upon him, the right to start the next run from a vantage point: all, with no exception, compete under the same conditions, at any stage or tier of the game. Not so in market contests, where the winner of the first stage is quite often able to bend to his advantage, in an endogenous way, the rules of the game. (Economic history is rich in examples of this kind. We need but to recollect how

monopolies and oligopolies developed in the course of time). Furthermore, the really alarming news about the *new economy* age – the economy
of knowledge and information – is the appearance of a new kind of
competition: *positional* competition as it was called by the late Fred
Hirsch. The central feature of positional competition is the generation
of "winner-take-all" outcomes, the so-called "superstar effect," as the
American economist Shermin Rose called it. It is easy to see that in
presence of positional competition equating across individuals initial
opportunities are of little or no avail.

The results are there for everybody to see: never to the same extent as
in the last two decades has one witnessed such an outburst of social
inequalities, both horizontal (among different social groups) and vertical ones (among one subject and another), at the same time as the world's
wealth has been growing at a pace never seen before. This is the great
aporia of the present model of development: extraordinary economic
growth (in the sense of sustained increases of wealth) and civil progress
(in the sense of wider and wider spaces of freedom for people) are unable to keep the same pace. (Oxford Review of Economic Policy 1999)
It is therefore easy to understand why, under such circumstances, an
increased affluence does not go hand in hand with greater public happiness. Indeed, limiting or even destroying the ability to partake in the
economic game for those subjects, which, for some reason, are left on
the market borders, while it adds nothing to the capabilities of the winners, it produces a rationing of freedom, which is always detrimental to
happiness.

In the third place, it is not true that the market is an institution compatible only with the egocentric motivations of its agents. It is not true
that market competition is generated *solely* by the self-interest of economic actors. This is not only factually untrue, as even casual observation will confirm, it is also theoretically reductive; and there is more to
it. The well-known interpretation of the market by Nobel Prize Ronald
Coase according to which the market is a more than perfect substitute
for the Smithian benevolence – in the sense that, reaching farther than
benevolence ever would, the market will achieve much more than the
latter does – is on close scrutiny untenable. Briefly, the reason is the
following. While acknowledging that in order to function the market
implies the practice of benevolence and compliance with the code of
commercial morality by all agents, Coase claims that market outcomes
depend only on the self-centered interest of participants. Which is tant-

amount to saying that in order to exist and perform well, the market needs certain virtues to be practiced by economic agents, but such practices have no bearing on the outcomes themselves of the market process because outcomes ignore those practices altogether: a patent paradox. Why ever should rational subjects practice virtues like benevolence or sympathy if the effects of market interaction were totally independent of such virtues? (One should remember that, unlike what happens with a carce resource, the use of a virtue accumulates it, and vice versa).

It is true instead, that given certain conditions which I will elucidate in paragraph 5, the market can become a means to strengthen the social bond, both by promoting wealth-distribution policies that make use of its mechanisms (instead of operating outside of it as is the case with redistribution carried out by the State), and by providing an economic space in which those values such as trust and solidarity upon whose existence the market itself depends, can be put into practice and therefore reproduced. In other words, this means to assert that there exists a variety of models of market societies, each of them compatible with one specific culture – seen as a body of values shared by agents. And it also means that the problem of the choice of the market model (or of the way leading to one specific market model) is as (maybe even more), interesting and noble for organized civil society as the search for efficiency conditions of a given market model, in its turn an expression of one *given* culture. If I am right, this may be the ultimate meaning of the following passage by L. Einaudi:

> Having believed for a long time that the task of the economist was not to state aims for the legislator, but to remind that, whatever the goal pursued by politics, the devices adopted should be sufficient and appropriate, I am today wondering whether, and I may finally conclude that, the economist should not sever his duty as a critic of means from that of stater of purposes, *that the study of aims is part of the science by the same extent as the study of means to which economists limit themselves.* (Bresciani Turroni, Einaudi, 1942, pp. 15–16, Italics added).

4. The Limits of the Liberal-Individualistic Doctrine of Rights

Before I proceed, I find it proper to address the following question: what explains the centrality within economic theory of the thesis of the "naturality and inevitableness" of the "motivational supremacy" of what P. Wicksteed called non-tuistic self-interest, and therefore of the market as the forum of privatism? In order to answer, I must take up a position relating to the contemporary predominant version of liberal thought, the liberal-individualistic one. Liberalism is today the prevailing current in western political and economic thought. Origins, historical development and promises of this fundamental tradition of our cultural heritage are well known to all. Yet precisely this hegemonic position puts before liberal thought an unavoidable challenge, that of thoroughly clarifying the economic and social implications descending from its individualistic version, according to which the conception of right can be seen as independent of the relations linking human beings to one another. By denying the cogency of the notion of common good and by visualizing civil society simply as the sum of monad-individuals, this version proves incapable of accounting for the social character of rights, especially of those pertaining to the economic domain, and in so doing one cannot see how such version can be made compatible with Catholic Social Thinking.

In fact, according to liberal-individualism, a right cannot be fully made use of unless the subject involved is capable of negotiating his own interests with other subjects. As neo-contractualistic literature clearly shows, a peculiarity of people participating from the very beginning, in the social covenant, is their ability to pursue their own interests by unrestricted negotiations. Now it is certainly true that if contracting parties are somehow equal in their negotiating potential, the most efficient way for them to reach their goals is to be left free to negotiate with one another. But what about those who do not possess the same skills? As we know, the liberal-individualistic response is that they can be "represented," that is, their interests can be represented by some gifted subject during the negotiating process that brings the social contract into being. Summing up, an agent may be left out of the social contract if she lacks negotiating abilities or if no one accepts to represent her. This means that a subject is the holder of rights only as long as he is capable of pursuing his targets, directly or indirectly, as contracting party in some social pact.

As G. Grant subtly observes, the majority obtains equality in the distribution of social benefits as a result of having agreed to a social pact; notwithstanding this, such equality "will exclude liberal justice from those who are too weak to enforce contracts – the imprisoned, the mentally unstable, the unborn, the aged, the defeated and sometimes even the morally unconforming." (Grant, G. 1985, pp. 83–84.) What I wish to stress here is that in spite of the due emphasis laid on the category of rights by the individualistic version of liberal thought, its bare rendering of what it means to be a person deprives the concept itself of any practical significance, at the same time as it removes any justification of the acknowledgement of the moral rights of people.

This difficulty survives even in the re-thinking of liberalism as offered by John Rawls in his celebrated 1971 work. As we know, Rawls argues that the constituents (those who choose the principle of justice in an original position and behind the veil of ignorance) are certainly rational, free and equal beings (here emerges the evident Kantian inspiration), yet they are rational only insofar as they are in a position to choose the principles of justice from behind the veil of ignorance and on the basis of self-interest. On close examination, the weakest side to the neo-contractualist theory is precisely its limited range of applicability. The persuasive force (in both moral and economic sense) of liberal-individualism is largely due to its affinities with the contract in the domain of positive right. In the latter context, the agreement between parties is evidence that what the parties consider to be their interest represents the definition of what is just and – as long as one is prepared to accept the principle of the sovereignty of individual preferences – even of what is good. Undeniably, such an argument possesses very interesting peculiarities while exerting great intellectual appeal. On close examination however, it will appear to be somewhat thin.

First of all, the contract traditionally governs relations of exchange of equivalents. Now, if no one can ever doubt the relevance of exchange relations, especially in an age, like ours, characterized by globalization, it is likewise true that they do not exhaust the wide range of relations among subjects. One has but to think of pure conflict relations such as the ones related to problems of distributive justice; or of coordination relations, namely those from which social conventions and norms develop. The pretension to examine similar relations under the species of the contract would not only impair our comprehension of how a democratic social order can be achieved, but it would also raise a moral question of great momentum. In fact, if agreement among the parties were to be the fundamental criterion of what is just, or even of what is good, indeed not a few daily-life situations would completely escape moral control. As in the celebrated case of the prisoner's dilemma, we may well agree upon something considered evil by any moral theory other than the one that defines what is right or good in terms of what is susceptible of agreement.

After all the point I raise here is that a satisfactory theory of rights can but acknowledge the social quality of rights. It follows that the individualistic theory of rights that claims to assimilate the attribution of rights to the process by which individuals pursue their targets, is inadequate because its vision of the concept of person denies precisely what is essential to a person: interaction with others and the relationship to others as a value *per se*. So much so that, within the perspective in question, market coordination of given individual preferences is seen as an essentially amoral process, even though some subjects, endowed with lesser negotiating power, may be to some extent left out of the benefits of this process. (Sen, A. 1993, pp. 519–541; Inman, R. 1987)

To quote but one example, let us think of what actually happens when contracts are incomplete, i.e. when their enforcement entails recourse to endogenous strategies such that the positions of power initially enjoyed by some subjects enable them to modify to their advantage the rules of the game. Actually in such cases, which are becoming more and more frequent, the market ceases to operate as a mechanism merely allocating resources, to be turned into a power-regulating mechanism.

In view of all this, how can one imagine (or hope) that asocial individuals will ever accept to conform to the rules of some kind of social order? The liberal-individualistic answer is that the market can aggregate individual preferences in an agnostic way, i.e. independently of any specific notion of common good. Yet we know this to be true only in presence of considerable homogeneity in individuals' preferential orderings, as K. Arrow demonstrated long ago in his famous impossibility theorem in social choice. This is tantamount to saying that market as an institution cannot reconcile "basic conflicts"; it is not capable of leading to any kind of social order starting from the mere consideration of individual preferences (or tastes). It should be remarked that the difficulty in settling "basic conflicts" is not to be found in the market as such – this was the mistake of a large portion of Marxism that engendered the belief that the abolition of the market would suffice to attain a superior social order. That difficulty instead lies in the pretension to base a cooperative decision process – like the market – simply by aggregating individualistic preferences through procedures and incentive schemes of an extrinsic nature.

The argument above can be summed up by saying that the individualistic version of liberalism entails a juxtaposition of what one may call libertarian individualism and institutional guarantism. On the one hand,

extreme intransigence is advocated for public morality (it is not sufficient to abide by the laws of economic life, it is also required to sub-
scribe to the principle of the supremacy of what is just over what is
good, just as J. Rawls did in his celebrated *A Theory of Justice*). On the
other hand, one advocates the maximum subjectivism within the private
sphere, that is to say, as far as individual preferences are concerned.
This is the very root of the problem of mutual compatibility plaguing
that version: how can the concept of arbitrarily individualistic preferences, *per se* unrelated to the relational dimension, conciliate with the
idea that society's institutional structure should offer guarantees for such
preferences to be satisfied? How can one expect individualistic preferences to receive "protection" at social level?

All things considered, the ultimate difficulty posed by the liberal-
individualistic set-up is too narrow a concept of freedom: freedom merely
as self-determination, as mere opportunity for free choice (*free to choose*
is Milton Friedman's vivid expression). One cannot deny that the essence of freedom lies in the actual practice of that power represented by
the act of choosing. However, as M. Botturi indicates, the subject does
not only have the *power* to choose, it also *needs* to choose. (Botturi, M.
1998) Choosing is a function of needs not to be neglected and which
must be met. Actual economic subjects do not choose just for the sake
of doing so, but in order to reach profitable goals. It is a fallacy to believe that flesh-and-bone persons may find satisfaction in self-determination alone. Indeed, freedom is not just an opportunity to choose, it is
also the ability to do so, and it is *self-realization*. This implies that self-
determination is to serve the attainment of those objectives which the
subject considers worthy, – in one word, happiness-bringing. As A. Sen
and others have recently clarified, rational choice is a function of the
agent's realization. Freedom here has a positive sense as in I. Berlin, and
positive freedom is not such unless it entails the relationship to the
other. Not only does freedom as self-realization has to take into account the other's freedom (as the liberal-individualistic thought also
recognizes), but it has a deep, vital need for the other. It is the relation
with the other which is crucial to freedom, not the relation *to* others
per se. As it was well expressed by authors participating in *Controversy* about "Economy and happiness" in the 1997 issue of *Economic
Journal*, happiness is the central issue in economic science, more so
than utility. "Economic matters are of interest only insofar as they make
people happy" (Oswald, 1997, p. 1815). But happiness is a relational

concept, unlike utility, which is an individualistic concept. Robinson Crusoe may maximize his own utility, by himself, but for him to be happy there must be Friday.

A remarkable foretaste of the idea that there is no happiness outside of life within society is found in Antonio Genovesi. In his *Discourse about the true purpose of letters and sciences* (1754) – a true manifesto of Neapolitan Enlightenment – Genovesi wonders why Naples, albeit well inhabited, well placed for trade, well gifted with bright minds and rich talents, and so on, is not so developed a nation as others in Northern Europe. Genovesi's prompt answer is that Naples lacks "love for the public good." He actually writes: "The primary support of civil society, the most important of all, is love for the public good, which can preserve these societies in the same way that it made them. Societies where private interest reigns and prevails, where none of their members is touched by love of the public good, not only cannot reach wealth and power, but also if they have already reached them, are unable to maintain this position." (Bruni, L. and Sugden, R. 1999)

Finally, while liberal-individualism proves its inability to embody the perspective of EHR, this is not the case with liberal-personalism as a doctrine, which adopts the intrinsic value of the human person as the objective basis for the attribution of rights. (Wojtyła, K. 1979)

5. Civil Economy as a Way to Humanize the Market

One wonders: given today's situation, is it reasonable to expect the fulfillment of a humane model of market economy? Close observation tells us that this question involves the dimension of freedom, viewed however not simply as self-determination, but above all as personal realization in the sense explained above. In this second, wider-ranging meaning, a free society presents features quite similar to those of the decent society mentioned by Margalit. (Margalit, A. 1996) Society is decent when its institutions do not humiliate its members, which is the case when it grants benefits and services to its citizens but at the same time denies them their dignity, which is precisely what happens when their "preferences" are rejected or their opinions neglected. It is well-known that today the most devastating humiliation, hence hindrance to self-realization, is economic irrelevance. Feeling useless (we are thinking of *lift boys* or of the holders of "socially useful jobs") is even more mortifying than feeling exploited, also because the awareness of exploitation almost invariably generates some kind of reaction among the exploited, hence a structural change, whereas humiliation produces resignation, thus perpetuating the status quo. This is why a free society is one, which aims at acknowledging in each person the ability to act, not just to do. (*Agere* is altogether different from *facere*, as K. Wojtyła convincingly stressed in our times in his *The acting person*). For this reason it is important to recognize each person's right to act, as Aquinas noted already in his time.

Well, a positive answer to the question that opens this paragraph presupposes the fulfillment of one specific condition: the creation *inside* the market (not outside it), until the critical threshold has been reached, of an economic space composed by subjects (such as those I will mention shortly) *modus operandi* is based on a value system which is being nurtured by the realization of economic activities themselves. Since participation in these activities cannot be severed from its originating culture, it belongs to that principle of economic behavior, which is called reciprocity. Unfortunately, the principle of reciprocity is often mistaken for that of the exchange of equivalents, so much so that it is opposed to the principle of gratuity or gift. Elsewhere, (Zamagni, S. 1997, 1999b, 1999c) I have dwelt upon a description of the essential differences between the principle of the exchange of equivalents underlying the sphere of private economy, and the principle of reciprocity underlying the sphere of civil economy. I will just highlight the main feature of reciprocity, namely the fact that the transfers it originates are inseparable from human relations: the objects of transactions cannot be separated from the identity of those who originated them. Because of this, exchange ceases to be anonymous and impersonal. Literature offers evidence that in reciprocity equilibrium it is possible to give without loosing and to take without removing. This is, essentially, the meaning of the civil economy project. (The expression "civil economy" first appeared in the political economy vocabulary in 1753, when the University of Naples established the first-ever chair in economics, appointing Antonio Genovesi to hold it).

To avoid any misunderstanding let me make it clear that I have no intention of maintaining that human behavior is steered solely by intrinsic reasons (such are the motives descending from the moral constitution of agents). I simply mean that such motives *contribute* towards explaining human behavior and, more specifically, that they are an essential item in the definition of its rational norms. Even less I want to assert the possibility of governing a modern economy by the sole principle of reciprocity as opposed to the principle of exchange of equivalents. My belief is rather that a market organization capable of stimulating pro-social behaviors instead of depressing them, will tendentially operate more efficiently (since it will substantially reduce transaction costs), and above all in a more "feliciting" way for everybody.

Briefly, the point is: man *per se* is not basically or exclusively individualistic, as axiological individualism has it; or exclusively "socializing," as axiological holism claims. Man will instead tend to develop those inclinations that are most incentivated in the social context in which he happens to operate. The thesis that pro-sociality and reciprocity are "exceptions" and as such can be explained in the light of the "natural and historical supremacy" of self-interest, appears as extreme as the opposite one. In his absolute behavioral complexity, man may be driven by a variety of motivational configurations. In a complex market society, efficiency and justice will then result from the society's ability in exploiting the *best* individual motives, leaving economic agents free to strive at one time for their own and for others' maximum well-being. The continuing mediation between the diverse motivations, which is required, obviously implies "enlightened self-interest" but is not exhausted in it. That is why I find reductionist, hence unacceptable, the stance taken by Nobel Prize George Stigler when he writes:

> I arrive at the thesis that flows naturally and irresistibly form the theory of economics. Man is eternally a utility-maximizer – in his home, in his office (be it public or private), in his church, in his scientific work – in short, everywhere. He can and often does err: perhaps because the calculation is too difficult [...] what we call ethics, on this approach, is a set of rules with respect to dealings with other persons, rules which in general prohibit behavior which is only myopically self-serving [...] Let me predict the outcome of the systematic and comprehensive testing of behavior in situations where self-interest and ethical values with wide verbal allegiance are in conflict. Much of the time, most of the time in fact, the self-interested theory [...] will win. (Brennan, G. and Buchanan, J. 1981, p. 158)

How widespread is, in reality, the practice of reciprocity? Surprisingly enough, even casual observation will suggest that this is a widespread phenomenon in advanced societies. It does operate in various forms and at different levels, within the family, in small informal groups, in volunteer associations. But there is more to it: the transaction network supported by reciprocity as leading principle can be found in all undertakings, from cooperatives – in which reciprocity takes the form of mutuality – to nonprofit organizations in which reciprocity flows into utter gratuitousness, to the firms making up the "economy of communion." (Bruni, L. 2000) Empirical evidence of the economic results achieved so far by civil economy and its practical implementation is ample and very accurate and I will not dwell on it here. Let me just mention, as many studies on economic development have emphasized, that in order to function the so-called "new competition" model requires at the same time an inclination to cooperate on the part of agents, and a close-knit network of transactions, with a structure very similar to the structure of reciprocity relations. As a matter of fact, this is the secret of so many success stories in Italian industrial districts and in emerging countries.

For all the above reasons it does not make sense, nor does it help, to raise the problem of the choice between the principle of reciprocity and the principle of the exchange of equivalents. It does not make sense in that no indisputable standard is available on which one could base one's choice. For sure, the criterion of Pareto efficiency cannot provide such a standard because, for obvious reasons, this notion of efficiency does not apply to a system of economic relations supported by the principle of reciprocity. It does not help – in fact; it is detrimental – because an advanced economy needs both principles to be implemented. An attempt to base successfully all kinds of transactions on the culture of the exchange of equivalents is naive. Should such vision become predominant, individual responsibility would coincide simply with what has been agreed upon in a contract. Everybody would then take care only of what they are "in charge of," with grotesque consequences that it is easy to imagine. If the culture of the exchange of equivalents and that of reciprocity do not merge, the system's growth potential will be impaired; hence the urgent need to get the sphere of civil economy off the ground. Free competition between private economy and civil economy – both competing under equal conditions – will then decide which goods or services agents consider to be more conveniently provided according to the principle of the exchange of equivalents, and which goods or services are to be produced according to the principle of reciprocity. Without paternalism of any sort.

6. Concluding Remarks

The ultimate sense of the argument developed above is that the search for a way to humanize the economy contains a demand of relationality, which one should carefully investigate and satisfy at best if one wants to dispel perverse effects of great magnitude. Indeed, how good the performance of an economic system is depends also on whether certain conceptions and ways of life have achieved dominance. As a growing number of economic scholars over the past couple of decades – to cite but a few: K. Arrow, A. Sen, B. Frey, R. Sudgen, R. Frank, P. Dasgupta, S. Kolm – have tenaciously stressed, economic phenomena have a primary interpersonal dimension. Individual behaviors are embedded in a preexisting network of social relations, which cannot be thought of as a mere constraint, as mainstream economists continue to believe. Rather, they are one of the driving factors that prompt individual goals and motivations. It seems to me that the central problem in the current transition towards a post-Fordist society is to understand how to fare so that individuals may be at liberty to decide the procedures for the supply of the goods they demand. What is at stake here is not so much freedom to decide the overall *composition* of goods to be produced (more of private *versus* more of public goods; more merit *versus* more relational goods), but freedom to decide *how* that composition should be achieved. This is why one cannot advocate the efficiency principle in order to decide *what* and *how* to produce. Undiscriminating admirers of the market as a social institution seem to overlook the fact that it is the very hegemonic expansion of those relations that I called private economy, that will slowly but inexorably destroy the whole system of social norms and conventions which constitute a civil economy, thereby paving the way for the success of new forms of statism. Today it is urgent to admit that the hypertrophic growth of both State and private market is a major explanation of the many problems that embarrass our societies. Such being the situation, the solution cannot be found in the radicalization of the public economy *versus* private economy alternative, or neo-statism *versus* neo-liberalism, but in a healthy flourishing of those forms of organization that shape a modern civil economy.

The most obnoxious consequence of a narrow-minded (and obsolete) notion of market, still predominant to this day, is to lead us to believe that a behavior inspired by values other than non-tuistic self-interest inexorably drives economy to disaster. By encouraging us to expect the worst of others, such vision eventually brings out the worst in us. Moreover, in the end it immensely hampers the exploitability of such inclinations as trust, benevolence, reciprocity, since that vision perceives these inclinations as merely inborn peculiarities of human nature, unrelated to the civilization process in progress in our societies. As Wolfe points out with great insight referring to the sphere of the relations that shape private economy:

> [...] The problem with reliance on the [private] market as a moral code is that it fails to give moral credit to those whose sacrifices enable others to consider themselves freely choosing agents. By concentrating on the good news that we can improve our position, rather than the not-so-good, but socially necessary, news that one might consider the welfare of others as our direct concern, the market leaves us with no way to appreciate disinterest. (Wolfe, A. 1989, p. 102.)

Since motivations sustaining the principle of reciprocity are motives whose fulfillment is at least as legitimate as the fulfillment of self-interested motives, a truly liberal society should not prevent beforehand – that is, at the level of institutional design – the growth and dissemination of the former to the detriment of the latter, as is foolishly happening today. In the absence of actual – not just virtual – competition among different subjects of supply of the various categories of goods, the citizen-consumer will be left with a reduced space of freedom. One might end up living in a more and more affluent society, more and more efficiently inundating us with commodities and services of all sorts, but more and more "indecent" and, ultimately, desperate. Indeed, the reduction of human experience to the "accountancy" dimension of utilitarian calculus is not just an act of intellectual arrogance; it is disclaimed by actual experience in the first place.

One final remark. We know that by the rules of reason alone one can rationalize the existing, but cannot invent much. In fact, in order to invent one needs to cast a sketch of sense beyond customary rationality. It seems to me that for this task those who experience in their lives a relational dimension of the sense of time are better equipped than those who live within an enlightened utilitarian dimension which is certainly capable of bringing to scientific certification, much less so to scientific creation. This is perhaps the most significant contribution of EHR to the overcoming of reductionism (Zamagni, S. 2000) so massively present in today's economic theorizing – a reductionism which is a major impediment to innovation of economic ideas and to the enlargement of the scope of economic research. It is a fact – often ignored – that the early history of the discipline was characterized by the centrality, within the economic discourse, of the happiness category. Political economy was essentially seen as the "science of happiness." It was only with the marginalistic revolution of the second half of 19th Century that the category of utility completely superseded that of happiness. Since then, economics managed to be referred to as the "dismal science."

This paper reproduces with minor changes and amendments the essay of the author published in Boswell, J. S., McHugh, F. P. and Verstraeten, J. (eds): *Catholic Social Thought: Twilight or Renaissance?* XXII–300 p., by permission of Peters Publishers.

The Possibility of Stakeholder Capitalism

R. Edward Freeman
Darden Business School
University of Virginia
USA

Much has recently been written about the concept of *stakeholders* or *stakeholder capitalism*. More heat than light has been generated in an attempt to counter the current wave of restructurings, rightsizings, downsizing, smartsizings or whatever the current management buzzword is for layoffs. This debate rests on several misunderstandings about the idea of "stakeholders" and the very basics of capitalism and its moral foundations. In an attempt to juxtapose the rhetoric of the right (presumably in favor of shareholders) with the rhetoric of the left (presumably in favor of stakeholders) a false choice has been given to executives.

Background

The idea of stakeholders is quite old, growing up in the 1960s through the work of management theorists Eric Rhenman, Igor Ansoff, Russell Ackoff and their students. And the idea is connected to a very old tradition that sees business as an integral part of society rather than an institution that is separate and purely economic in nature.

Identifying and analyzing stakeholders was originally a simple way to acknowledge the existence of multiple constituencies in a corporation. The main insight was that executives must pay some strategic attention to those groups who were important to the success of their corporation. So far ...common sense.

As the pace of change accelerated in business, these thinkers and others began to advocate more interaction with stakeholders so that they had some sense of participation in the day-to-day affairs of the corporation. So we had the emergence of consumer advisory panels, quality circles, just-in-time inventory teams, community advisory groups and so on, all designed to get the corporation more in touch with the key relationships that affect its future.

During the 1980s the idea of "stakeholder management" was articulated as a method for systematically taking into account the interests of "those groups, which can affect and are affected by the corporation." Again ...just good management.

During the late 1980s and early 1990s we also saw the emergence of a strong movement concerned with business ethics. Much of the business ethics movement has been rooted in a response to perceived corporate excesses such as oil spills, financial scandals and business-government collusion. But a small number of thinkers began to ask questions about the very purpose of the corporation. Should the corporation serve those who own shares of stock or should it serve those who are affected by its actions?

The choice was laid bare: corporations can be made to serve stockholders or they can be made to serve stakeholders.

False Choice

Most thoughtful executives know that this choice between *stockholders* and *stakeholders* is a false one. Corporations must be profitable at rates determined by global capital markets. No longer can executives ignore the fact that capital flows freely across borders and that rates of return are more complicated than internally generated hurdle rates and payback schemes. Business today is truly global.

Most thoughtful executives also know that great companies are not built by obsessive attention to shareholder value. Great companies arise in part out of a shared sense of purpose among employees and management. This sense of purpose must be important enough for individuals to expend their own human capital to create and deliver products and services that customers are willing to pay for.

We need only return to the wisdom of Peter Drucker and W. Edwards Deming to see the importance of meaning and purpose and the destructiveness of fear and alienation in corporate life.

Management thinkers such as Tom Peters, Charles Handy, Jim Collins and Jerry Poras have produced countless examples of how employees, customers and suppliers work together to create something that none of them can create alone. And capital is necessary to sustain this process of value-creation.

From Cadbury to Volvo, Nordstrom to Hewlett-Packard, executives are constantly engaged in intense stakeholder relationships. Boeing's building of the 777 jet involved a complex process of interaction among suppliers, customers and employees. The interests of stockholders and stakeholders are often aligned rather than in conflict. Stockholders are a key stakeholder group whose support must be sustained in the same way that customer; supplier and employee support must be garnered. The issue is one of balancing the interests of these groups.

Furthermore, in a relatively free political system, when executives ignore the interests of one group of stakeholders systematically over time those stakeholders will use the political process to force regulation or legislation that protects themselves.

Witness the emergence of "*stakeholder rights*" in the US in the form of labor legislation, consumer protection legislation, environmental (community) protection legislation and even shareholder protection legislation.

There are many ways to manage a successful company. Daimler Benz will be different from Volvo. Procter and Gamble will be different from Unilever. However, all will involve the intense interaction of employees with critical stakeholders.

The more that stakeholders participate in the decisions that affect them, be they product design decisions or employment contract decisions, the greater the likelihood that they will be committed to the future of the corporate enterprise.

Four Principles

Business today is different. Capital markets have been liberalized and are truly global. For the most part, investment flows to the best returns regardless of geography just as customers buy the best value regardless of country of origin.

Political regimes have been liberalized so that everyone is adopting some version of capitalism or market mechanisms, yielding the possibility for unprecedented worldwide growth. And incredibly powerful information technologies tie together sophisticated communications systems that make McLuhan's concept of a global village a stunning reality.

Business approaches this century of change with an ideology that can only be called radically shop-worn and outdated. As businesses change the composition of human society, its ideology proclaims that it is amoral, that business ethics is an oxymoron that it is only doing what shareholders require.

Furthermore, it captures the imagination by claiming that this is a result of our human drive to compete. Business is to be understood as warfare and executives are the lonely soldiers on the battlefield of global markets. The result of this myth of the primacy of the shareholder and the view of business as *"cowboy capitalism"* leads to a public mistrust and misunderstanding of the processes that make companies successful.

Stakeholder capitalism, properly formulated, is the new story that we need. But stakeholder capitalism is not a leftist excuse to regulate business nor is it a convenient whipping boy of the right to avoid common moral decency and fair play. Stakeholder capitalism has to serve as a model of the very best companies – the best that business can be; that should be our expectations for corporations.

Let us begin by defining the primary stakeholders as customers, suppliers, employees, financiers and communities. Managers simply have to pay attention to the concerns of these groups. Fully articulated stakeholder capitalism will have to add models of relationships with other groups such as the media, government, competitors and even terrorists.

Stakeholder capitalism should be based on four principles.

A. Stakeholder co-operation

Value is created because stakeholders can jointly satisfy their needs and desires. Capitalism works because entrepreneurs and managers put together and sustain deals or relationships among customers, suppliers, employees, financiers and communities. And the support of each group is vital to the success of the endeavor. This is the co-operative common sense part of business that every executive knows, although the myth of the primacy of the shareholder tells us that some stakeholders are more important than others.

But try building a great company without the support of all stakeholders. It simply cannot be sustained.

B. Complexity

Human beings are complex creatures capable of acting from many values. Sometimes they are selfish and sometimes they act for others. Many values are and shared. Capitalism works because of this complexity rather than in spite of it.

C. Continuous creation

Business as an institution is a source of the creation of value. Co-operating with stakeholders and motivated by values, business people continuously create new sources of value.

This creative force of humans is the engine of capitalism. And the beauty of the modern corporate form is that it can be made to be continuous rather than destructive. One creation does not have to destroy another. Rather there is a continuous cycle of value creation that raises the well-being of everyone. People come together to create something, be it a new computer program or a new level of service.

D. Emergent competition

Competition emerges from a relatively free and democratic society so that stakeholders have options. Competition emerges out of the co-operation among stakeholders rather than being based on the urge to "get the other guy."

Competition is important in stakeholder capitalism but it is not the primary force, as so many business thinkers claim. Humans' urge to co--operate and create is what distinguishes us from apes, not our urge to compete.

Stakeholder capitalism does not pretend to be amoral like its cowboy cousin. It takes a firm ethical stand: that human beings are required to be at the center of any process of value creation; that common decency and fairness are not to be set aside in the name of playing the game of business and that we should demand the best behavior of business.

Stakeholder capitalism is no panacea. It simply allows the possibility that business becomes a fully human institution.

Stakeholder capitalism bases our understanding and expectations of business not on the worst that we can do but on the best. It sets a high moral standard, recognizes the common sense practical world of global business today and asks managers to get on with the task of creating value for stakeholders.

There is much work to be done to articulate stakeholder capitalism in a way that allows business to occupy the moral high ground. Seeing business as anything less than an institution that is a vital part of our conception of the good life gives away too much.

Adam Smith understood that business and ethics must go together. He wrote *The Theory of Moral Sentiments* along with *The Wealth of Nations*. Stakeholder capitalism can be a way of resuscitating what we have forgotten about Adam Smith and of building a capitalism that is human.

Reprint of R. Edward Freeman's paper "Mastering Management: Understanding Stakeholder Capitalism" *Financial Times*, July 19, 1996.

Effectiveness, Efficiency, and Ethicality in Business and Management

Wojciech W. Gasparski
Institute of Philosophy and Sociology
Polish Academy of Sciences
Warsaw, Poland

Humans are distinguished from other things not for being doers but for being capable of acting rationally, in a morally right or wrong way, i.e. for being able to use knowledge to do good or evil. In short, we are (sometimes) rational moral agents. A nonhuman animal may do another good turn, but not nearly as rationally, hence effectively, as a human. And an intelligently programmed robot may behave rationally (by proxy) but not with good or evil purposes – except again by proxy – for it is incapable of having intentions of its own. This is not to say that man is the only rational and ethical animal. But, among all the animals known to us, we are certainly the ones capable of acting in the most rational and right way – as well as the only ones capable of putting the highest reason in the service of evil.

(M. Bunge, *Treatise on Basic Philosophy*, p. 323)

1. Introduction

This paper could, following the fashion for repeating titles and adding consecutive numbers to them, be called "*Human Action in Business: Praxiological and Ethical Dimensions Two*," because this is the English title of the "One," i.e. the fifth volume in the series *Praxiology: The International Annual of Practical Philosophy and Methodology* (1996).

The series began with the volume *Praxiologies and the Philosophy of Economics* (1992) presenting the output of the first international conference in the discipline's history organized on such a great scale in

Warsaw in 1988. The conference was attended by such eminent scholars as Herbert A. Simon and Kenneth E. Boulding. The conference presented the achievements of not only the Polish school of Praxiology, created by Tadeusz Kotarbiński, but also the Austrian school, created by Ludwig von Mises. This was the first open presentation in a Central European country of the achievements of Austrian praxiology, on which the theory of economics characteristic of that school was founded, a theory that was critical of a centrally planned economy, the criticism stemming from praxiological considerations.

As Mises writes:

> The essential mark of socialism is that one will alone acts. It is immaterial whose will it is. The director may be an anointed king or a dictator, ruling by virtue of his charisma, he may be a Führer or a board of Führers appointed by the vote of people. The main thing is that the employment of all factors of production is directed by one agency only. One will alone chooses, decides, directs, acts, and gives orders. All the rest simply obeys orders and instructions. Organization and a planned order are substitutes for the 'anarchy' of production and for various people's initiative. Social co-operation under the division of labor is safeguarded by a system of hegemonistic bonds in which a director peremptorily calls upon the obedience of all his wards. [...] In terming the director society (as the Marxians do), state, government, or authority, people tend to forget that the director is always a human being, not an abstract notion or a mythical collective entity. We may admit that the directors or the board of directors are people of superior ability, wise and full of good intentions. But it would be nothing short of idiocy to assume that they are omniscient and infallible. [...] In a praxiological analysis of the problems of socialism, we are not concerned with the moral and ethical character of the director. Neither do we discuss his value judgments and his choice of ultimate ends. What we are dealing with is merely the question of whether any mortal man, equipped with the logical structure of human mind, can be equal to the task incumbent upon a director of a socialistic society. [...] The answer to the question is of course is "no" just because of praxiological reasons, i.e., because of the principal impossibility. And this is the argument – it is impossible even if: "We assume that the director has at his disposal all the technological knowledge of his age [...] but [...] he must act. He must choose among an infinitive variety of projects in such a way that no want which he himself considers more urgent remains unsatisfied because the factors of production required of its satisfaction are employed for the satisfaction of wants which he considers less urgent. (Mises, L. von 1968, pp. 695–697)

The involvement of management in the problems defined by norms of efficiency and ethicality is obvious to authors of textbooks. For example, there is a book of *Management* by R. W. Griffin which defines the concept of management as follows: management is a set of actions comprising planning and decision-making, organizing, leadership, i.e.

managing and controlling people, directed at an organization's resources (human, financial, material and informational) and carried out with the aim of fulfilling the organization's objectives in an efficient and effective way (Griffin, R. W. 1996, p. 38). Thus, by definition management is linked to praxiological norms, i.e. *effectiveness* and *efficiency*. We consider the primary task of praxiology to be the construction and justification of norms concerning efficiency. (Kotarbiński, T. 1995)

As for ethical norms in relation to management, Griffin says they belong to management ethics, which comprises norms of behavior followed by individual managers in their work. (Griffin, R. W. 1996, p. 137) But are things really as simple as they seem from the above? "The human inclination for making overall assessments has been mentioned more than once. It is clear that we do not want to see the positive things about our opponents or any blemishes in the ideological orientation to which we are emotionally tied. We want to wholeheartedly love or hate, admire or condemn [...]" (Ossowska, M. 1970)

Is management actually managed by norms or imperative elements of ethical and moral systems on the one hand, and praxiological systems on the other, present in the form of commands and prohibitions? Are they like traffic codes saying how to move around the roads and byways of managing organizations of every kind? Or are they a businessman's Decalogue? Bookstore shelves and, to a greater degree, the stalls of street vendors are loaded with numerous volumes promising success "as long as you obey." What? Norms?

Freeman and Phillips write

> It is both ironic and appropriate that a paper on stakeholder theory should appear in a volume that adds "ethics" to the traditional foci of praxiology: "efficiency" and "effectiveness." The primary impetus behind the development of stakeholder theory has been the addition of ethics to the traditional concentration on the theory of the firm on issues of efficiency and effectiveness directed towards the maximization of shareowner value. Like praxiology, economics began as a branch of philosophy. Adam Smith, widely considered as the father of modern economics, was Professor of Moral Philosophy at University of Glasgow. So too did the Polish branch of praxiology begin and develop as a branch of philosophy due to the influence of Tadeusz Kotarbiński. Scholars of economics, however, have placed some distance between their field and its origin in ethics and moral philosophy. Many influential economists consider their work amoral or at least feel that the "invisible hand" of the free market renders unnecessary considerations of morality in economic theory and practice. [...] Scholars of praxiology may fruitfully take the points of this paper as both a warning against the self-imposed limitations within praxiology's most highly developed branch (i.e., economics) and as constructive re-

commendations for improving future research into praxiological issues through inclusion and consideration of the vital "third E." (Freeman, R. E. & Philips, R. A. 1996, pp. 65–66).

2. The Praxiological and Ethical Dimensions of Human Action

The American Foundation for Economic Education has just published the fourth edition of Ludwig von Mises' *Human Action: A Treatise on Economics*, in which Mises outlines the praxiological foundations of human economic activity as follows.

> For a long time men failed to realize that the transition from the classical theory of value to the subjective theory of value was much more that the substitution of a more satisfactory theory of market exchange for a less satisfactory one. The general theory of choice and preference goes far beyond the horizon, which encompassed the scope of economic problems. [...] It is much more than merely a theory of the "economic side" of human endeavors and of man's striving for commodities and an improvement in his material well being. It is the science of every kind of human action. Choosing determines all human decisions. In making his choice man chooses not only between various material things and services. All human values are offered for option. All ends and all means, both material and ideal issues, the sublime and the base, the noble and the ignoble, are ranged in a single row and subjected to a decision which picks out one thing and sets aside another. Nothing that men aim at or want to avoid remains outside of this arrangement into a unique scale of gradation of preference. The modern theory of value widens the scientific horizon and enlarges the field of economic studies. Out of the political economy of the classical school emerges the general theory of human action, praxiology. The economic or catalactic [= science of exchanges, Whately, 1831] problems are embedded in a more general science, and can no longer be served from this connection. No treatment of economic problems proper can avoid starting from acts of choice; economics becomes a part, although the hitherto best elaborated part, of a more universal science, praxiology. (Mises, L. von 1966, p. 3)

It was in connection with this work that Hayek, a former student of von Mises wrote:

> It has often been suggested that [...] economics and the other theoretical sciences of society should be described as "teleological" sciences. [...] But the term remains nevertheless misleading. If a name is needed, the term *praxiological sciences*, deriving from A. Espinas, adopted by T. Kotarbiński and E. Slutsky, and [...] clearly defined and extensively used by Ludwig von Mises [...] would appear to be the most appropriate. (Hayek, F. A. von 1952, p. 45)

Praxiology defines action as the behavior of a person undertaken consciously and in accordance with that person's will, with the aim of causing a desired state called the objective of the action. Actions in a praxiological sense are actions carried out individually, or single-subject actions. Multiple-subject behavior and the behavior of collective subjects is not action in a praxiological sense. In a praxiological sense, these are systems of single-subject actions displaying a structure resulting from praxiological laws. Action is the fundamental (ultimate) feature of the human that Mises calls *Homo agens*.

Praxiology is indifferent to the ultimate objectives of actions. Its discoveries concern all kinds of actions, irrespective of the intended objectives. It is the science of the means, not the end. It uses the concept of happiness in a purely formal sense. In praxiological terms, the premise that happiness is a particular human objective is a tautology. It does not imply any statement on the state of things that would ensure that happiness.

> There are phenomena which cannot be analyzed and traced back to other phenomena. They are ultimate given. [...] Human action is one of the agencies bringing about change. It is an element of cosmic activity and becoming. Therefore it is a legitimate object of scientific investigation. As – at least under present conditions – it cannot be traced back to its causes, it must be considered as an ultimate given and must be studied as such. (Mises, L. von 1996, p. 17)

Economic activity is an arena of practical human activity *par excellence*. The concept of *practicality* – as defined within the philosophy of practicality – applies to the activity in question. According to which practicality is defined by the three "Es," the first two being praxiological values, and the third "E" comprising ethical values. As I wrote some time ago:

> [...] "practicality," synonymous with "efficacy" [...] is the fundamental technical value of action. More precisely, it is the general name for those values, which are thus also called the practical values of action. The evaluation of actions from the point of view of practicality (efficacy) is by nature non-emotional, inter-subjective. The evaluation concerns the result of the action (the effect) on the one hand, and the action itself (the process) on the other. [...] Actions receive the quality of practicality to a greater degree the more effective and/or efficient they are. (Gasparski, W. 1987–1988)

Effectiveness and efficiency are economic values. *Effectiveness* refers to the result of the action, or its effect. *Efficiency*, on the other hand, refers to the efficacy of the action itself, or the process of change. Effectiveness and efficiency appear as values that are economic *sensu stricto* when they can be measured in monetary units, and they are economic values *sensu lato* when they are of a qualitative nature. Contrary to economic values ethical values are qualitative.

Economic and ethical values in an analytical sense are independent of each other. This means that whenever we analyze any human action, methodological accuracy requires that this be done independently. That is why Kotarbiński constructing his praxiology, Mises creating his praxiology or Espinas proposing his praxiology created it as an amoral area, free of ethical valuations, but not as something anti-ethical, as their prejudiced adversaries criticized. Thus, praxiology is not unethical, but analytical when it studies the conditions of the effectiveness and efficiency of actions. The task of praxiology – as Kotarbiński said it – is nor propaganda, neither it is the glorification of an action as being the most practical, but an impassive presentation of its features.

> The ultimate goal of human action is always the satisfaction of the acting man's desire. There is no standard of greater or lesser satisfaction other than individual judgments of value, different for various people and for the same people at various times. What makes a man feel uneasy and less uneasy is established by him from the standard of his own will and judgment, from his personal and subjective valuation. Nobody is in a position to decree what should make a fellow man happier. [...] Praxiology is indifferent to the ultimate goals of action. Its findings are valid for all kinds of action irrespective of the ends aimed at. It is a science of means, not ends. It applies the term happiness in a purely formal sense. In the praxiological terminology the proposition: man's unique aim is to attain happiness, is tautological. It does not imply any statement about the state of affairs from which man expects happiness. (Mises, L. von 1966, p. 14–15)

On the other hand, economic and ethical values in a synthetic sense, namely in the sense of the quality of human actions expressed by these values, are dependent on each other in the sense that each is a non-eradicable axiological context of the other.

An intention that is the noblest possible in an ethical sense will not be accomplished without a minimum of effectiveness and efficiency in action. The most effective but morally reprehensible action loses its practical value in a culture that defines norms of moral acceptability, or justness. Virtue (the Greek *arete* and Roman *virtus*) is a cultural norm of practice agreed upon in a synthetic sense. It applies to an effective action undertaken towards a just objective. The focus here is not only on the ultimate goal of the undertaking, but also on the intermediate goals (the means), which includes the methods of conduct.

> Although ethical values must be complemented by praxiological values, the two kinds should not be confused. Efficiency can serve any purpose [...]. It is good to be efficient in good; it is evil to be efficient in evil. The same is true in economics. We cannot help Adam without adopting sound economic proce-

dures. Economics without the ethical goal of minimizing suffering may be neutral ethically, but when it helps the rich at the expense of the poor it is evil. (Hiż 1992, p. 428)

Regardless of whether a person is a businessperson, a CEO, or a lower-level manager, or performs the simplest duties, he or she acts in accordance with the practical situations of which he or she is the subject. Each such a situation comprises the niche of its subject. The practical situation of any actor is determined by the facts that this subject distinguishes from among other facts due to the subject's values. Values provide facts with meaning, based on which the subject considers them satisfactory or not. If a practical situation is unsatisfactory to the subject, the actor aims to change the facts in a way that will enable him or her to obtain a satisfactory situation. However, even when the actor considers the situation to be satisfactory, change is necessary. This time it is not a therapeutic change that is involved, but a preventive one that will serve to prevent any violation of the satisfactory situation by natural and human--induced processes. The first kind of change concerns the interior of the practical situation, while the second kind concerns the situation's context – the "reminder of the world."

Modern praxiology considers "action being," or the reality linked to action in categories of the ontology of practical situations. (Gasparski, W. 1994) According to Mises:

> Man's freedom to choose and to act is restricted in a threefold way. There are first the physical laws to whose unfeeling absoluteness man must adjust his conduct if he wants to live. There are second the individual's innate constitutional characteristics and dispositions and the operation of environmental factors; we know that they influence both the choice of the ends and that of the means, although our cognisance of the mode of their operation is rather vague. There is finally the regularity of phenomena with regard to the interconnectedness of means and ends, viz., the praxiological law as distinct from the physical and from the physiological law. (Mises, L. von 1996, p. 885)

3. Business Activity as Serious Action

Józef Maria Bocheński, a Polish philosopher linked to the University of Frieburg, introduced the differentiation between thinking and serious thinking. The latter is thinking the objective of which is knowledge, a cognitive value. (Bocheński, J. M. 1992, p. 16) It seems that a similar concept should also be introduced to differentiate between action and action that is aimed at economic value. Thus, economic action would constitute serious action. In both cases, seriousness is measured by positive values of the effectiveness dimensions of the action. Seriousness also requires that the social axiological context of actions be taken into consideration, under pain of any of them being considered unacceptable in a given culture.

The analysis of human actions in terms of the "triple E" is the condition for the highest-ranking seriousness of these actions – wisdom. Wisdom is the technique that refers to the strong character of the acting subject. Praxiology, says Bocheński, is one of those disciplines in which we can find assertions corresponding to the injunctions of wisdom. Finally, let us note that the English adjective "businesslike" includes "serious" among its meanings.

In a lecture delivered to the Sixth Polish Philosophical Congress in Toruń in 1995, I proposed the following computer metaphor. The order of action programs treated seriously is as follows: first comes the operational program, or a praxiological "action DOS," in accordance with Mises' regularity laws concerning the relations between means and objectives. The next program is one that provides an ethical insight into actions, of which it can be said that it helps determine Boulding's goodwill factor (Boulding, K. E. 1985a); this program is a kind of action Windows. Finally, there is the program for carrying out the subject's intention, or an action "word processor," or in our case a program of responsible economic activity as described by Elaine Sternberg (1966).

Thus, the task of business ethics is not that of a missionary, converting business "cannibals" to economic vegetarianism. Its task is to (at least) point out the fact that besides those who assume the perspective of morally indifferent business activity, there are also those – quite numerous, even among business people – who see the necessity of taking into account the moral framework of that activity. This is a social fact, and ignoring it is nothing short of crime, it is a mistake! It is an error in the art of doing business *par excellence*, i.e. economic activity that is serious (businesslike). Moreover, when appearing on the market in the role of a rival or a consumer, even the morally indifferent (as he sees himself) businessman wishes other business people with whom he associates to display "common decency," and not to oppose "distributive justice" – as referred to by Sternberg.

This role dilemma is resolved sensibly within at least a pair of actions, in which the same subject appears on the market in one role and then in another. The task of business ethics does not consist in "ruining" business, but similarly to the practice of critics of air pollution by car exhaust fumes, in installing catalytic converters.

Referring to Kotarbiński's concept of "small philosophy," one can say that business ethics viewed as described above is a "small ethics of economics." Small, because it does not aspire to create an Arcadia of economic life; small, because it realistically aims at business civilization, i.e. its professionalization. And, one cannot be professional without obeying the norms of the profession, both the praxiological ones (i.e. the technical norms in the sense of Espinas' *technologie generale*) and those that turn people in a given profession into a group of colleagues in the true sense of the term, i.e. in terms of ethical standards.

Finally, let us note that action programs constitute contexts for each other. One can use an ethical program within a praxiological framework, and reach for the praxiological DOS within the ethical framework – to retain the computer metaphor. This mutual conceptualization is similar to a hermeneutic circle: one program appears in the light of the other. This creates the possibility of correcting the objectives and means by replacing their linear correlation with the circular correlation of a systemic approach, at the same time providing protection against relativism. This arrangement of action programs is the result of studying human behavior, or serious thinking about it and wisdom stating that "ethics must be effective" while virtue requires effectiveness in achieving a just objective. (Gasparski, W. 1996c)

4. The Problem of Rationality

Human action is undertaken in the world of the acting subject's practical situations. The subject chooses the state of things – the objectives that he or she aims for. Prompted by *techne*, the subject chooses the means he believes will allow him to achieve the goal. In doing so, he always behaves rationally within the limits defined by every person's personal qualities and routines learned previously that could be updated in specific action. Things look different from the point of view of the observer, who is not the subject of the criticized action and expresses his judgment on how he, the observer, would act if he were in the subject's position.

> When applied to the ultimate ends of action, the terms rational and irrational are inappropriate and meaningless. The ultimate end of action is always the satisfaction of some desires of the acting man. Since nobody is in a position to substi-

tute his own value judgments for those of the acting individual, it is vain to pass judgment on other people's aims and volitions. No man is qualified to declare what would make another man happier or less discontented. The critic either tells us what he believes he would aim at if he were in the place of his fellow; or, in dictatorial arrogance blithely disposing of his fellow's will and aspirations, declares what condition of this other man would better suit himself, the critic. [...] We applied to the means chosen for the attainment of ends, the terms rational and irrational imply a judgment about the expediency and adequacy of the procedure employed. [...] An action unsuited to the end sought falls short of expectation. It is contrary to purpose, but it is rational, i.e., the outcome of a reasonable – although faulty – deliberation and an attempt – although an ineffectual attempt – to attain a definite goal. The doctors who a hundred years ago employed certain methods for the treatment of cancer, which our contemporary doctors reject, were – from the point of view of present-day pathology – badly instructed and therefore inefficient. But they did not act irrationally; they did their best. It is probable that in a hundred years more doctors will have more efficient methods at hand for the treatment of this disease. The will be more efficient but not more rational that our physicians. The opposite of action is not *irrational behavior*, but a reactive response to stimuli on the part of the bodily organs and instincts that cannot be controlled by the volition of the person concerned. [...] It is fashionable nowadays to find fault with the social sciences for being purely rational. The most popular objection raised against economics is that it neglects the irrationality of life and reality and tries to press into dry rational schemes and bloodless abstractions the infinite variety of phenomena. No censure could be more absurd. Like every branch of knowledge economics goes as far as it can be carried by rational methods. Then it stops by establishing the fact that it is faced with an ultimate given, i.e., a phenomenon which cannot – at least in the present state of our knowledge – be further analyzed. (Mises, L. von 1966, pp. 19–21)

In response to the search for socio-economic rationality, the Swiss academic Peter Ulrich (1996) has proposed a three-level concept: constitution, system and action. The constitutional level involves the political and economic order concerning the laws and procedures of social communication. This order would define the normative integration of society and the means of overcoming social conflicts, providing the economy with ethical legitimization (the ethical rationality of communication). The system level involves the structure of ownership rights and rules of competition ensuring the economic system's functional integration, defining ways of dealing with complexity, i.e. effectiveness on the system scale (functional rationality). The human action level involves "private" business activity and commercial transactions taking into account personal integrity and prosperity, defining ways of dealing with the limitations of resources, i.e. efficiency on the system scale (calculations of rationality related to the strategy of conduct and personal responsibility).

According to Sternberg, business is a well-defined professional economic activity, the goal of which is the maximization of the value that the longer-term results of that activity, i.e. the sale of goods or services, hold for the owner. This value is called the owner value. In this case, of course, we are talking about value expressed in monetary units, or financial value. This goal and no other defines an organization, firm, company, etc. as a business; any other objectives realized by a given organization are either means (intermediate goals) of achieving the principal goal, or are additional goals resulting from the fact that the organization is not only a business, but something else as well, e.g. it collects taxes, provides financial assistance to social programs, etc. (Sternberg, E. 1994).

Differentiating between a business and a non-business is functional and not objective; this differentiation is praxiological *par excellence*, because it refers to the goal of the action. The rationality resulting from Sternberg's teleological concept concerns behavior at the third level – the level of action. "Business is ethical when it maximizes long-term owner value subject to distributive justice and ordinary decency. If an organization is not directed at maximizing long term owner value, it is not a business; if it does not pursue that definitive business purpose with distributive justice and ordinary decency, it is not ethical." (Sternberg, E. 1996, p. 60)

A goal-based approach to doing business provides a basis for the analysis of the praxiological and ethical dimensions of company operations and allows to assess the degree to which this approach can be used outside the economy to analyze other kinds of serious (*businesslike*) activity. The size of the present paper does not allow expanding this concept, which well deserves a separate presentation.

> The immanent principal goal of an industrial enterprise is.production. [...] besides its principal goal it also has other immanent goals, such as survival, expansion and rationality. [...] These observations also allow for better insight into the function – and thus the ethics – of the entrepreneur. According to the traditional approach, he is often perceived as a representative of the capitalists and no one else. In actual fact the entrepreneur represents the industrial enterprise as a whole, regardless of the industrial enterprise's constitution. It has been said over and over that there is no such thing as a "saintly entrepreneur," or a "saintly manager." [...] this is not true. The ideal entrepreneur stems from the structure of an industrial enterprise – a person who unselfishly, and if necessary against everybody else, serves the industrial enterprise as a whole. And we know that there have been great entrepreneurs in history who remained faithful to that ideal. (Bocheński, J. M. 1993)

Maximization of owner value, i.e. the value belonging to the stock-holders, supported as it is by praxiological and moral arguments, is criti-cized – also from praxiological positions – by advocates of the theory of corporations that refers to the concept of stakeholders. (Freeman, R. E. & Phillips, R. A. 1996) This concept, akin to the division into the core, the outer ring and the environment of an organization introduced in early sixties by a Polish praxiologist Jan Zieleniewski, dates back to the time when the Stanford Research Institute introduced the name *stakeholder* in 1963, as a pun on the word *stockholder* and a counterbalance to the word *shareowner*, as the person whose increasing wealth the company's operations were meant to serve.

5. The "Triple E" in Religious Perspective

Presenting the issue of the correlation between business and religion, Donald G. Jones (1982) notes that the Jewish and Catholic religions have traditionally given consideration to economic and professional ethics. More than 30% of the Talmud covers issues of business ethics, and a lot of time is devoted to fairness, reliability and honesty in business at rabbinical and Talmudic schools. The Catholic Church has developed a theological and ethical approach to money, work and business relations. In Medieval mon-asteries and universities, moral casuistry formed the core of the education program. Issues such as just prices, just wages, cultivating production and reliability in business were the subjects of moral philosophy and theologi-cal reflection. Puritan ministers constantly presented "cases of conscience," many of which referred to the mercantile economy. In the 19th century, the ethical dimension of the industrial revolution was expressed in numerous sermons, treatises, homilies, articles and books. However, the debate be-tween the creators of the "gospel of wealth" and the "Christian socialists" did not result in any significant contribution to the theology of economics, nor did it bring a systematic ethics of modern business.

In the 20th century, apart from a few works by Catholic academics dealing with business ethics, the contribution to business ethics of peo-ple teaching religion has been modest, according to Jones. He mentions three approaches to business ethics when characterizing American theo-logians: the social gospel, Christian social realism, and the so-called gospel of wealth.

The first approach refers to the critics of progress and opponents of big business from the early 20th century. In the 1930s it drew from socialist ideology, supporting trade unions, perceived business as the main secularizing force in society, seeing giant corporations as the source of corruption and injustice, and the development of business ethics as the legitimization of something that should not be legitimized. In view of this, teaching business ethics was considered anti-effective, serving the development of business while hampering the restructuring of democratic capitalism.

The second approach recognizes individual interests as a fact of economic life, but demands that they be controlled by political factors. It considers state regulation and strong trade unions to be the means of introducing moral norms on the market. This approach focuses on social and political ethics (issues of war and peace, human rights, minority rights); business ethics is a marginal interest for supporters of this approach. "Under conditions of a modern highly advanced society, the system of a social market economy with an economic and social policy adjusted depending on the situation, seems to be the best way of protecting a good that is rare in the economy, namely morality. " (Dylus 1994)

The tradition of the gospel of wealth is very strong in America. It defends the free market and the identification of Christian morality with economic success. The search for arguments supporting capitalism and opposition to socialism is a constant feature of this approach. In the modern version of this approach we have neo-conservatism, represented by Michael Novak and Seymour Siegel who deal with the theology of economics. They – similarly to Freeman and Phillips – refer to the works of Adam Smith, believing like he did that wealth is an ethical value because creating wealth leads to decreasing poverty and increasing prosperity. For this reason, political interference with market operations is unethical, because it disturbs the mechanism of the market's functioning. Many neo-conservatives consider the teaching of business ethics to be harmful because it is hostile towards business.

Jones thinks it is time for a fourth approach, in which theological reflections move down from the macro level to the micro level, or the level of practical problems that managers face in their careers, and offer them advice. This, however, requires the clergy to acquire knowledge allowing for dialogue with business people. Studies have shown that American clergymen are unable to advise managers in numerous practical situations involving moral and praxiological dilemmas. Only about 10% of clergymen are able to talk competently with business people.

Therefore, Jones believes, clergymen should be encouraged to acquire knowledge on management and market economics. Clergymen should be able to use the language of business ethics, talk about ethics issues in connection with management not in the language of religion, but in a language comprehensible to managers. It would be advisable for clergymen to learn the techniques of ethical analysis and decision-making if they are to advise managers on how the latter should act when making decisions.

This is the only way clergymen can develop partnership relations with the managers who need their advice, without usurping a monopoly on moral issues. "We will not increase our trust in matters of business ethics among managers," writes Jones, "unless we improve our instruments of judgment." Thus, clergymen should study the works of philosophers of morality, and this could be an unpleasant prospect for some clergymen, ads Jones, if they are encouraged to learn about lay ethics. "My own view – says Jones – is that ethics is universal, and prior to Judaism and Christianity. Whatever one's conviction on this issue, the Christian tradition offers a strong historical warrant for "doing ethics" as an autonomous function of practical reason. Surely this was true for Aquinas, who learned moral philosophy from Aristotle, and for Luther, who, when advising tradesmen, magistrates, and princes, relied on stoic philosophy as well as Aristotle. Furthermore, if pastors can do therapeutic counseling while employing methods, words, and insights from Freud, Horney, Jung, Erikson, and Rogers, they can likewise do ethical counseling while drawing on the theories and language of secular philosophers and teachers of business ethics." (Jones, D. G. 1982, p. 223.)

I think a good example of this approach can be found in numerous addresses by Pope John Paul II to business people, published in the United States in a volume edited by R. G. Kennedy (1994). Extensive excerpts from these addresses were quoted in *Human Action in Business: Praxiological and Ethical Dimensions*.

> Business today needs a broad and updated professionalism; in other words, a professionalism which is above all "qualified." As the experts say, we must move away from a "job-centered professionalism" towards a "process-centered professionalism." That presupposes not only a serious competence in the area of one's own specific task, but a cultural sensitivity as well, which allows one to take stock quickly of technological progress and to gear up for it in a quick and effective way. In short, what is needed is professionalism with a wealth of operational qualities, but also rich in the human, social, cultural and ethical values which make work gratifying as well as productive.

Furthermore, professionalism in business must always be inspired by a "person-alist" vision which has at heart the "human factor," above all before all else. Estimates and analyses are certainly necessary, along with statistical checks and technical certification; the "philosophy of total quality" is also important for a continuing improvement of the product. But a business must be especially committed to respect the primacy of the human being over work and work itself over technology, profit and capital. "To humanize" companies means, therefore, to place the human person in a privileged position by eliminating special inter-ests, which often enough harm the community; it means to draft solutions to prob-lems in the light of basic ethical values that remain perennially valid. This presup-poses the attempts by business leaders and employees to engage in a serene and constructive dialogue with the goal of foreseeing and resolving conflicts and dis-agreements with ultimately harm the well-being of all. (John Paul II 1996, p. 150)

A similar view is presented by Dennis P. McCann from DePaul University in Chicago, who believes that business ethics is an important area of praxiological reflection on the challenge posed by the knowledge society. This praxiological perspective for the analysis of ethical issues resulting from the use of knowledge on a social scale should, according to McCann, stem from recognition of the importance of the religious dimensions of change.

The lessons for the peoples of Eastern Europe is not that American Catholics are to be envied for having become just like their neighbors, only more successful. The American Catholic experience provides reasonable hope that the economic anxieties generated by the changes currently underway in Eastern Europe can become an opportunity for praxiological development, religious and moral, as well as political, social and economic. [...] Catholic social teaching's capacity for critical engagement should be developed praxiologically as a resource for business ethics that is open to all persons, regardless of their ethnic back-ground or religious orientation. It is a part of humanity's common moral legacy to the 21st century. (McCann, D. P. 1996)

The work of Yvon Pesqueux and Bernard Vergniol consider the atti-tude of Protestants towards the "triple E," especially in France. Accord-ing to these authors,

[...] business ethics is first and foremost the ethics of efficiency. The more civi-lized a society is, the greater the degree of moral awareness in the companies operating within it. It is not the task of the companies to develop a morality for the rest of society, because only free and democratic social institutions can do that. It is the duty of political institutions to define moral rules as it is of compa-nies to obey them and to respect the public interest by which they are strictly limited. (Pesqueux, Y. & Vergniol, B. 1996)

Presenting the Indian ethos, S. K. Chakraborty encourages readers to replace aspiration towards success with ambition for perfection, which creates a promising chance for combining human values and the practice of human action. The Indian Institute of Management in Calcutta, which refers to religion both and the teachings of Gandhi promotes this attitude.

As concerns the approach characteristic of Judaism in its attitude towards business, Meir Tamari from the Center for Business Ethics in Jerusalem points out that Judaism is largely a system of laws combined with religion. For this reason, though the Jewish community uses the term business ethics, it would be more appropriate to speak of forbidden actions and obligatory actions. These two kinds of action are defined and recommended by the two trends of divine laws and spirituality, justice and integrity characteristic of Judaism.

6. Cultural Factors

In their work "Praxiology: Components of Managerial Action in a Diverse Working Environment" Samuel M. Natale and Mark B. Fenton (1996) discuss issues of ethical and effective decision-making by managers. Similar issues in India are presented by Theophane A. Mathias, who lists the commonly followed ethical norms in that country. The most important norm, however, is the Praxis Norm. The latest studies show that this is the most important basis for recognizing behavior as being ethical. This is the case probably because there is no universal moral code, while the variety of religions practiced in India hampers ethical valuation. Hence, saving face is an important criterion. The issue is similar, or maybe even goes further, in China and Japan, where praxis or public opinion is the basis of moral judgment.

Ethical leadership in a free society was the subject of a lecture by John A. Matel, who made insightful references to the Polish reality.

> According to surveys, many Poles do not trust business people. They sometimes talk as if business is something akin to organized crime – writes John A. Matel – that business men and women make money by avoiding rules, stretching the truth to the breaking point and cheating poor people out of their hard-earned money. Poland's history partially explains this attitude. Throughout the 19th century, when free markets and free enterprise were developing in Western Europe and the United States, Poland was occupied by powers that viewed markets with varying degrees of suspicion. More recently, Communists were actively hostile to the very idea of free markets. In their propaganda, they tried to demonize the free market, associating with it all kinds of capitalistic evil, and actively sought to prevent open development of any market they could not control. However, nobody, not even the most determined despots, can completely repeal the laws of supply and demand. Evens under the harshest conditions markets develop.

Communist Poland was no exception. A non-official market always existed in Poland, sometimes it was quite sophisticated, but it was inefficient, illegal, and underground shadow of a true free market. [...] How can it be a surprise that "biznesmeni" (a Polish equivalent to English *businesspeople*) were perceived of as crooks and confidence men. Business tends to attract marginal people. To make things work, business people were forced to rely on questionable practices, since, in the absence of market triggers and discipline of freely agreed prices, bribes and manipulation provided the only incentives to buy or sell. One of the most egregious of Communism's many sins was to make criminals out of ordinary business people, engaged in making a living, and strip them of their ability to act ethically. Only under free conditions can business people, or anybody else, act ethically. Doing the "right thing" presupposes a choice between doing the "right thing" or doing the wrong thing. (Matel, J. A. 1996, pp. 245–246)

A Finnish philosopher Olii Loukola, who lectures on business ethics in the Baltic States, has shared his knowledge of the experience of those countries in terms of competing with the rules of liberalism and morality.

In fact the only countries where the market systems are closest to a workable *laissez faire* system, have always had solid and stable background institutions; that is, a long history of more or less interventionist institutions and a background moral conduct. It is only through a lengthy period of experiment and established institutions in history that the general trust has been created. This construction of general trust results from reciprocal fair interaction between individuals and institutions. When it comes to the post-soviet countries this means that one cannot just go and implement a *laissez faire* system in any of these countries and expect it to work, when this central background institution is missing. (Loukola, O. 1996, pp. 295–296)

Marie Bohata, a scholar from Prague, deals with similar issues when she discusses certain aspects of the economic transformation in the Czech Republic. "After the 'Velvet Revolution' in the Czech Republic, an overwhelming majority of the population agreed to create the foundations of a capitalist system as quickly as possible, disregarding the character of business practices." She identifies three origins of the existing unethical practices: a heritage of the past regime and its specific way of thinking and behavior; phenomena connected specifically to the transformation period with "new opportunities" and temptations which it brings; new phenomena related to the market system itself. As an optimist she believes "that most of these bad practices are of temporary nature and we may hope to get rid of them, or at lest weaken them, by means of better laws, growing market experience, and education. Many entrepreneurs and 'would-be-entrepreneurs' sought to get rich quickly and to take advantage of new opportunities while they lasted. However, at present we can already observe some changes in public opinion, some signals of growing social and ethical awareness and sensitivity." (Bohata, M. 1996, pp. 299–300)

Culture is like gravitation, says the author of one of the fundamental books on business culture and management, you cannot experience it until you jump up (Trompenaars 1993). Immersed in our own culture, we generally fail to notice the conditions that depend on the systems of values accepted by other people in their business and other behavior. Contact with the cultures of other people and other cultures bring an awareness of the importance of that axiological context.

The internationalization of business, the very real globalization of economic life, has brought to the fore the issue of finding a common axiological denominator for stakeholders from different cultural backgrounds, different religious or philosophical beliefs. This has led to attempts at formulating the basic rules of business activity. The most promising attempts seem to be: *Caux Roundtable Principles for Business* (the name comes from the small Swiss town of Caux-sur-Montreux, where in 1986 Frederick Philips, former president of Philips Electronics and Olivier Giscard d'Estaing initiated meetings of people interested in reducing tensions in international trade), and *The International Business Ethics Code for Christians, Moslems and Jews* (accepted at a meeting held in Amman in 1993, ending a series of consultations by representatives of the monotheistic religions started in 1984 under the patronage of Prince Philip).

7. Conclusion

The paper discussed not so much the economic and ethical norms concerning management, or those that managers face in practice, but rather the fundamental premises and convictions related to the formulation of those norms and to behavior in various practical situations. Organizational culture is the space of common values of an organization's members, and thus cannot be enforced by supporters of other cultures. The culture of the society in which the organization functions is the culture of that society, so it should not be enforced from the outside. A given society is a business society in Boulding's sense only to the degree in which its members share values linked to exchange as the organizing factor, integration as the cohesive factor, and threat as the factor counteracting deviations.

Particular teams, particular organizations, professional societies and corporations have different ways of formulating definitions of the va-

lues they accept. *Organization and Human Systems Development (OD-
-HSD)* [Gellermann, Frankel & Ladenson 1990], which is a kind of super-code, is an example of an extensively developed collection of norms.
In this super-code, which includes an extensive commentary, we can
find the praxiological values of effectiveness, efficiency and alignment.
Effectiveness refers to achieving the desired results (objectives, visions,
missions, etc.), efficiency refers to the relation between desired results
and costs, while alignment refers to the degree to which the organization's desired objectives (giant arrow) are co-coordinated with the expectations of the organization's members (small arrows).

The super-code also includes (basic) ethical principles, moral norms
and ideals as well as a definition of conditions for deviation from the
norms. The basic rule is a paraphrase of Kant's categorical imperative;
it says that one should act with the awareness that the acting subjects
will live in the conditions that result from the effects of their actions.
Moral norms focus on the minimization of damage and wrong (do not
harm, do not kill, do not cause pain or injury, do not deprive of freedom,
do not deprive of pleasure, do not lie, do not cheat, do not break promises, obey the law, do not neglect your duties).

If deviation from the ethical norms is necessary to reduce harm or
fulfill ideals, it is permissible, according to the super-code, as long as
the moral grounds are presented. This is probably what Father Bocheński
had in mind when he wrote that "there is sometimes a contradiction
between the injunctions of morality and the injunctions of wisdom,"
and therefore "human life is most often a compromise between morality
and wisdom." "It seems," Bocheński concludes, "that due to this, most
people live according to a dual 'morality:' one authentic, the other based
on wisdom" [Bocheński 1994].

Thus we have come close to a concept as yet unmentioned, T. Kotarbiński's practical realism [1987, pp. 124–133]. As a reminder, a practical realist is someone who: (1) has a level-headed perception of the
world, (2) takes as the starting point that which currently exists, (3) respects the conditions of actions and the limits of their possibilities, (4) ac-
curately sets the hierarchy of priorities in his considerations when defining the directives for actions and plans [Pszczołowski 1991]. However, this is not a set of ideals forced upon anyone.

> In any case, issues of ethics by their nature are characterized by certain flexibil-
> ity. They cannot accept solutions that are too remote or too detailed. It is so easy
> then to fall into casuistry. One has to be aware of the main direction, have a kind

of compass, and resolve the executive issue, the application of an overall trend to current cases with their complex intertwined circumstances, specifically for each such case as a whole, in its fullness and the whole of its specificity. [...] Ethics is] not the whole answer to the question of how to act in order to deserve respect and not deserve the contempt of people worthy of respect. When trying to become aware of these answers and formulating them, it is of course a good thing to turn to books for advice, to have friendly talks with those who have gone through similar misery. Thus, let us read the authors of ethical delibera-tions, let us study works in which thinking in terms of ethics has found its strong expression [...] But let us not think that we will find guidelines as well defined, as well inter-subjectively justified as the theorems in algebra or geometry text-books. Independent ethics is independent also in the sense that one's own voice of conscience cannot be replaced by another persons' ones. In essence, each one of us, regardless of anyone else, refers chiefly to our own conscience. It is for each of us the supreme judge. On every matter, it issues a judgment that is harsh, inexorable, and final. (Kotarbiński, T. 1987, pp. 148–149) ·

Responsibility and Profit Making

László Zsolnai
Business Ethics Center
Budapest University of Economic Sciences
Hungary

> *If you want to make a profit please care about the world because we and other beings want to live in the same world.*
>
> (Public advertisement in London)

In a world that is ruled by giant multinational corporations producing large-scale environmental destruction and human deprivation, the conventional justification of profit making is not valid any more.
Social critique David Korten writes

> We are experiencing accelerating social and environmental disintegration in nearly every country of the world – as revealed by a rise of poverty, unemployment, inequality, violent crime, failing families, and environmental degradation [...] [Economic globalization] shifting power away from governments responsible for the public good and toward a handful of corporations and financial institutions driven by a single imperative – the quest for short-term financial gain. This has concentrated massive economic and political power in the hands of an elite few whose absolute share of the products of a declining pool of natural wealth continues to increase at a substantial rate. (Korten, D. 1996, p. 11. and p. 12.)

One of the most successful capitalists of our age, George Soros emphasizes that the financial success of an action cannot guarantee that the action was right. He writes:

in the social sphere what is effective is not necessarily identical with what is right, because of the reflexive connection between thinking and reality. [...] the cult of success can become a source of instability in an open society, because it can undermine our sense of right and wrong. That is what is happening in our society today. Our sense of right and wrong is endangered by our preoccupation with success measured by money. Anything goes, as long as you can get away with it. (Soros, G. 1997, p. 12.)

In the context of the contemporary global economy a *new form* of ethical and social justification of profit making is badly needed. Responsibility is central in providing criteria for *acceptable* business practices.

1. The Idea of Responsibility

German-American philosopher, Hans Jonas injected the idea of responsibility into the modern moral discourse. In his opus magnum *Das Prinzip Verantwortung* Jonas argues that the nature of human action has changed so dramatically in our times that this changed nature of human action calls for a radical *change in ethics* as well.

He emphasizes that in previous *ethics*:

[...] all dealing with the non-human world, that is, the whole realm of techne [...] was ethically neutral. (...) Ethical significance belonged to the direct dealing of man with man, including man dealing with himself: all traditional ethics is *anthropocentric*. [...] The entity of "man" and his basic condition was considered constant in essence and not itself an object of reshaping techne. [...] The effective range of action was small, the time span of foresight, goal-setting, and accountability was short, control of circumstances limited. (Jonas, H. 1984, pp. 4–5.)

According to Jonas new dimensions of responsibility emerged because *nature* became a subject of human responsibility. This is underlined by the fact of the irreversibility and cumulative character of man's impact on the living world. *Knowledge*, under these circumstances, is a prime duty of man, and must be commensurate with the causal scale of human action. Man should seek "not only the human good but also the good of things extra-human, that is, to extend the recognition of 'ends in themselves' beyond the sphere of man and make the human good include the care of them." (Jonas, H. pp. 7–8.)

For Jonas an imperative that is responding to the new type of human action might run like this. *Act so that the effects of your action are compatible with the permanence of genuine human life.* Or expressed negatively: *Act so that the effects of your action are not destructive of the future possibility of such life.* (Jonas, H. p. 11.)

Since *future human beings* and *non-human beings* do not have rights, our duties to future generations and to nature are independent of any idea of a right or reciprocity. Human responsibility is basically a *non--reciprocal duty* to *guarding beings.* (Jonas, H. pp. 38–39.)

Jonas states that the *necessary conditions* of moral responsibility are as follows. "The first and most general condition of responsibility is causal power, that is, that acting makes an impact on the world; the second, that such acting is under the agent's control; and the third, that he can foresee its consequences to some extent." (Jonas, H. p. 90.)

Jonas underlines the fact that prospective responsibility is never formal but always *substantive.* "I feel responsible, not in the first place for my conduct and its consequences but for the *matter* that has a claim on my acting." For example "the well-being, the interest, the fate of others has, by circumstance or by agreement, come to my care, which means that my control *over* it involves at the same time my obligation *for* it." (Jonas, H. 1984, p. 92. and p. 93.)

Jonas differentiates between *natural* responsibility, on the one hand, and *contractual responsibility*, on the other hand. "It is the distinction between natural responsibility, where the immanent 'ought-to-be' of the object claims its agent *a priori* and quite unilaterally, and contracted or appointed responsibility, which is conditional *a posteriori* upon the fact and the terms of the relationship actually entered into." (Jonas, H. 1984, p. 95.)

The *parent* and the *statesman* are presented as *ideal types* of natural responsibility and contractual responsibility, respectively. The *economic decision-maker* is somewhere in-between the role of the parent and the role of the statesman. For example, while a manager has a number of stakeholders (customers, employees, suppliers, creditors) with whom her or his company has contractual relationships, there are usually other stakeholders (the local community, the natural environment) which are affected by the company's operations but towards whom the company has no contractual, only a natural responsibility.

Jonas' theory of responsibility has important similarities with Carol Gilligan's understanding of *female morality.*

Conducting empirical studies at Harvard about the *moral experience* of *women*, Gilligan found that the morality of women is different from the morality of men. "Relationships, and particularly issues of dependency, are experienced differently by women and men. [...] The quality of embeddedness in social interaction and personal relationships that characterize women's lives in contrast to men's." (Gilligan, C. pp. 8–9.)

Gilligan reconstructs the morality of women as the *ethic of care*. "The ideal of care is thus an activity of relationship, of seeing and responding to need, taking care of the world by sustaining the web of connection so that no one is left alone." The ethic of care "is the wish not to hurt others and the hope that in morality lies a way of solving conflicts so that no one will be hurt." Women consider the inflicting of hurt as "selfish and immoral in its reflection of unconcern, while the expression of care is seen as fulfillment of moral responsibility." (Gilligan, C. p. 62, p. 65. and p. 73.)

Identity is construed differently by women and men. For *women* "identity is defined in a context of relationship and judged by a standard of responsibility and care. [...] Morality stems from attachment." For *men* "the tone of identity is different, clearer, more distinct and sharp-edged. [...] Thus the male 'I' is defined in separation." (Gilligan, C. pp. 160–161.)

Gilligan states that men and women represent *different moral ideologies*: the ethic of rights and the ethic of care, respectively. Separation is justified by an *ethic* of *rights* while attachment is supported by an *ethic* of *care*. "The morality of rights is predicated on equality and centered on the understanding of fairness, while the ethic of responsibility relies on the concept of equity, the recognition of differences in need. While the ethic of rights is a manifestation of equal respect, balancing the claims of other and the self, the ethic of responsibility rests on an understanding that gives rise to compassion and care." (Gilligan, C. p. 165.)

Table 1 shows the contrasting features of male and female morality.

Gilligan does not argue for the superiority of women's morality. She emphasizes the *complementary* of the *male* and *female ethics*. The two disparate modes of moral experience are connected in *mature morality*. "While an ethic of justice proceeds from the premise of equality – that everyone should be treated the same – an ethic of care rests on the premise of non-violence – that no one should be hurt." In maturity "both perspectives converge in the realization that just as inequality adversely affects both parties in an unequal relationship, so too violence is destructive for everyone involved." (Gilligan, C. 1982, p. 174.)

Gilligan's theory has great heuristic power. It suggests that the concept of responsibility should integrate both the *reverence* for *rights* and the *non-violence* of *care*.

TABLE 1
Male Morality versus Female Morality

male morality	female morality
separation	attachment
focus on rights	focus on needs
indifference	non-violence
justice	care
equality	equity
individual achievement	sustaining relationship

2. Responsibility in Economic Context

In economic context Kenneth E. Goodpaster presented the most advanced model of moral responsibility. (Goodpaster, K. E. & Matthews, J. B. 1982, Goodpaster, K. E. 1983)

Following William K. Frankena (1980), Goodpaster proposes to understand moral responsibility as a combination of two basic components, namely rationality and respect.

Rationality involves the following attributes:

(i) lack of impulsiveness;
(ii) care in mapping out alternatives and consequences;
(iii) clarity about goals and purposes;
(iv) attention to details of implementation.

Rationality described by attribute (i),…,(iv) radically differs from the rationality postulate of standard economics that identifies rationality with self-interest maximization under perfect knowledge of consequences.

The rationality concept used here is *process-oriented* and does not require maximizing anything. Max Weber's concept of 'goal rationality" and Herbert Simon's notion of procedural rationality are closely related to it. (Weber, M. 1921–1922, Simon, H. A. 1976, 1978)

Respect is the other component of moral responsibility.

> The moral point of view also includes a special awareness of and concern for the effects of one's decisions and policies on others, special in the sense that it goes beyond the kind of awareness and concern that would ordinarily be part of rationality, that is, beyond seeing others merely as instrumental to accomplishing one's own purposes. [...] This is respect for the lives of others and involves taking their needs and interests seriously, not simply as resources in one's own decision making but as limiting conditions which change the very definition of one's habitat from a self-centered to a shared environment. (Goodpaster, K. E. & Matthews, J. B. 1982, p. 134.)

Respect described in this way has a basic similarity to *altruistic behavior* that is widely discussed in economics. Stefano Zamagni offers a clear conceptualization of altruistic behavior. He defines individuals as altruistic "when they feel and act as if the welfare of others were an end in itself; that is, as something of relevance independently of its effects on their own well-being." If your concern for the welfare of others is merely instrumental for promoting your own longer-term ends and ceases once these ends can more easily be pursued in some other way, you are an enlightened self-interested person, not a genuine altruist.

Zamagni states the sufficient conditions of altruistic behavior as follows. A beneficial behavior is altruistic if it is actuated either by altruistic reasons only or by a mixture of altruistic and non-altruistic reasons when the former, in the absence of the latter, would have been sufficient to generate the beneficial behavior. (Zamagni, S. (ed.) 1995, p. xvi.)

To repeat, in Goodpaster's understanding moral responsibility is a combination of rationality and respect in the decision-making context. He writes:

> Rationality involves the pursuit of one's projects and purposes with careful attention to ends and means, alternatives and consequences, risks and opportunities. Respect involves consideration of the perspectives of other persons in the pursuit of one's rational projects and purposes. In the words of Kant, respect implies treating others, especially affected parties, as ends and not mere means. It implies a self-imposed constraint on rationality born of a realization that the worth of our projects and purposes resides in the same humanity shared by those who are likely to be affected by them. Taking the 'moral point of view' therefore, has both self-directed component (rationality) and other-directed component (respect). These, at least, provide us with an under-

standing of the spirit that underlines the concept of moral responsibility." (Goodpaster, K. E. 1983, p. 7.)

In Goodpaster's model "respect" is not an unambiguous notion. It reflects a mix of deontological and consequentialist considerations. I think that this mixed notion should be deconstructed to arrive at a more operationalised model of moral responsibility.

I propose to define respect as altruistic interest in the well being of the affected parties. In addition, I propose to introduce *deontological considerations* as a separate component into the model of moral responsibility. This separation of non self-interested motives has considerable support in the economic, psychological and sociological literature.

Jane Mansbridge refers to love and duty as the two basic forms of non self-interested motivation. (Mansbridge, J. 1990) Amartya Sen labeled this pair of motives as sympathy and commitment. (Sen, A. 1977) John Elster differentiates between altruism on the one hand and norm-following behavior on the other hand. (Elster, J. 1989) Christopher Jencks uses the terms empathy and morality. (Jenks, C. 1990) In their experimental study on co-operation Robyn M. Dawes, Alphons J. C. van de Kragt, and John M. Orbell refer to we-feeling and conscience in a similar way. (Dawes, R. M. et. al. 1990)

We can get a more robust model of moral responsibility by characterizing responsible decision making as a synthesis of deontological considerations, rationality in goal-achievement, and respect for the stakeholders.

I call this modified model of moral responsibility the *3 R model*, since *responsibility = reverence + rationality + respect*. This means that responsibility requires making decisions in a way that displays reverence for the applying norms, promotes the achievement of decision maker's goals, and shows respect for the affected parties.

3. Responsible Decision Making

In *complex decision situations* the following basic elements can be identified. At least two decision alternatives are available for the decision maker, that is, she or he can choose among different courses of action. In the decision situation ethical norms apply which represent duties of the decision maker. The decision maker has goals that she or he wants to achieve in the decision situation. Finally, different stakeholders are present that can be affected by the outcome of the decision.

We can formalize the above listed elements of complex decision situations as follows:

$$A_1,\ldots,A_i,\ldots,A_m \qquad (m \geq 2) \qquad (1)$$

This means that at least two *decision alternatives* are available for the decision maker.

$$D_1,\ldots,D_k,\ldots,D_p \qquad (p \geq 1) \qquad (2)$$

This means that at least one *ethical norm* apply in the decision situation.

$$G_1,\ldots,G_j,\ldots,G_n \qquad (n \geq 1) \qquad (3)$$

This means that the decision maker has at least one *goal* that she or he wants to achieve.

$$S_1,\ldots,S_q,\ldots,S_r \qquad (r \geq 1) \qquad (4)$$

This means that at least one *stakeholder* is present in the decision situation.

Responsible decision-making involves finding and implementing the decision alternative that best corresponds to the idea of responsibility in the given context.

Now we are in the position to pose the question: which is the appropriate rule for making a responsible decision.

$$A^* = \Omega \ (A_1,\ldots,A_i,\ldots,A_m) \qquad (5)$$

where A^* refers to the selected decision alternative.

We are searching for the decision rule Ω that selects the responsible course of action among the courses of action available for the decision maker.

Deontological pay-off is defined as the value of a decision alternative seen from the perspective of the applying ethical norms.

The deontological pay-off of the decision alternatives $A_1,\ldots,A_i,\ldots,A_m$ can be represented by a vector as follows:

$$d = [D(A_1),\ldots,D(A_i),\ldots,D(A_m)] \qquad (6)$$

It is natural that the decision maker considers the value of the decision alternatives from the perspective of the achievement of her or his goals. In classical decision theory this was the only dimension in which courses of action were evaluated and decided upon.

The goal achievement value of the decision alternatives $A_1,\ldots,A_i,\ldots,A_m$ can be represented by a vector.

$$g = [G(A_1),\ldots,G(A_i),\ldots,G(A_m)] \qquad (7)$$

The rational choice theory suggests that the decision maker is completely free both in selecting her or his goals and in weighting them. In fact, the decision maker is embedded in interpersonal relations and the social context. (Granovetter, M. 1985, Etzioni, A. 1988) So it is realistic to presuppose that the decision maker sets her or his goals and assigns weights to them in reference to those organizations and communities in which she or he happens to exist.

Stakeholders are present in complex decision situations and the decision alternatives render different pay-off for them.

The stakeholder pay-off of decision alternatives $A_1,\ldots,A_i,\ldots,A_m$ can be represented by a vector:

$$s = [S(A_1),\ldots,S(A_i),\ldots,S(A_m)] \qquad (8)$$

Stakeholders represent distinct "minds" in the sense of Gregory Bateson. (Bateson, G. 1979) However, it does not mean that for decision making purposes we cannot produce an aggregate assessment of the gains and losses of different stakeholders. If we use appropriate weights we can get a fair picture even using a compensatory model.

In contemporary moral philosophy different perspectives or viewpoints have been identified from which a decision or an act can be evaluated.

Amartya Sen distinguished between the viewpoint of the agent, the viewpoint of the observer, and the viewpoint of the agent as she or he sees herself or himself (doer relativity, viewer relativity, and self-evaluation relativity). (Sen, A. 1982, pp. 204–212.)

Holding (6), (7), and (8) together we can get a *multiple evaluation* of the decision alternative A_i.

$$v = [D(A_i), G(A_i), S(A_i)] \qquad (9)$$

The first component of the vector is the deontological value of the decision alternative, the second component is the goal-achievement value of the decision alternative, while the third component is the stakeholder value of the decision alternative.

The vector v represents a simultaneous evaluation of the same course of action from different perspectives. The deontological value is assessed from the perspective of an impartial observer, the goal-achievement value is assessed from the perspective of the decision maker, and while the stakeholder value is assessed from the perspective of the affected parties.

Amartya Sen introduced the concept of *goal rights systems* by which he means moral accounting systems where the fulfillment and non-realization of rights are incorporated in the evaluation of states of affairs. (Sen, A. 1982, 1983, 1985)

Sen lists the characteristics of the goal rights systems as follows:

> First, the goal rights system form a wide class rather than represent some unique moral position. There are many sources of difference, for example, what rights to include among the goals, in what form they are to be included, what non-right values (if any) are to be admitted, what weights to use, how should choice of actions be related to the evaluation of outcomes. Second, although rights are included within the evaluation of states of affairs, there could be other things to which the evaluation of states of affairs is sensitive in a goal rights system. The crucial issue is the inclusion of fulfillment and non-fulfillment of rights – rather than the exclusion of non-right considerations – in the evaluation of states of affairs. Third, while sensitivity of action-evaluation to consequences is essential for a rights-consequence system, such a system need not be fully consequentialist. Fourth, it may be worth emphasizing that, although a goal rights system incorporates a goal-included view of rights, it does not reject the instrumental relevance of rights either. (Sen, A. 1982, p. 199.)

The moral accounting system represented by (9) is a special sub-class of Sen's goal rights systems. However, there is an important difference. Our accounting system permits or even encourages the incorporation of those ethical norms that do not have corresponding rights while this is not permitted in the goal rights systems. In this sense it represents a broader category than Sen's goal rights systems.

The "responsibility calculus" advanced here, is very close to Sen's own ideal about the moral evaluation of acts. He wrote in his influential book *On Ethics and Economics*:

> To get an overall assessment of the ethical standing of an activity it is necessary not only to look at its own intrinsic value (if any), but also its instrumental role and its consequences on other things. [...] The advantages of consequential

reasoning involving interdependence and instrumental accounting, can then be combined not only with intrinsic valuation, but also with position relativity and agent sensitivity of moral assessment. (Sen, A. 1987, p. 75. and p. 77.)

A complete picture about the decision situation can be provided by a matrix that contains multiple evaluations of all the decision alternatives available for the decision maker.

$$V = \begin{matrix} D(A_1),\ldots,G(A_1),\ldots,S(A_1) \\ D(A_i),\ldots,G(A_i),\ldots,S(A_i) \\ D(A_m),\ldots,G(A_m),\ldots,S(A_m) \end{matrix} \qquad (10)$$

The matrix V may present incommensurability of different kinds for the decision maker as it was discussed earlier. Isaac Levi calls this situation unresolved value conflict in his treatment of "hard choices." (Levi, I. 1986)

Levis' proposal for making a choice under unresolved value conflict is that the decision maker should *prioritize* the conflicting values and then she or he can select the best alternative by using a *lexicographic* decision rule. That is, the decision maker should choose the decision alternative whose performance is the best according to the highest ranked value in the given situation.

In a complex choice situation the application of the lexicographic rule is rather unattractive or even counter-productive. It reduces the multidimensionality of the choice situation into one dimension. In the end the decision maker using the lexicographic rule deliberates her or his choice either as a deontological choice or a rational choice or an altruistic choice.

Another opportunity is to keep the complexity of the decision situation and try to find an *optimal compromise* among diverse value dimensions.

Trying to balance different values against one another is an essential strategy in complex choice situations. The *maximin* rule can do the required job quite well. It implies the maximization of the minimum payoff of decision alternatives.

Chess players intuitively know the maximin rule. However, it was first described by Austrian logician Ernest Zermello in 1912. The rule was developed further by the Hungarian-American mathematical genius, John von Neumann in his groundbreaking *Theory of Games and Economic Behavior* (Neumann, J. von & Morgenstein, O. 1944)

The rule of responsible decision-making is stated as follows:

$$A^* = \text{maximin } [D(A_i), G(A_i), S(A_i)] \qquad (11)$$

Responsible choice demands the selection of the *least worst alternative* in the decision space of deontological, goal-achievement, and stakeholder values, in the sense that the minimum value of the selected alternative is greater than the minimum value of any other alternative available for the decision maker in the given situation.

If there are two decision alternatives A_1 and A_2 then the responsible choice model requires the selection of A_1 if and only if

$$\text{min } [D(A_1), G(A_1), S(A_1) > \text{min } [D(A_2), G(A_2), S(A_2)]$$

The underlying principle of responsible decision-making is that the decision maker should find an optimal compromise among the applying ethical norms, her or his own goals, and the interest of the stakeholders.

The responsible decision-making provides a *Pareto optimal* result in the multidimensional decision space. This means that given the set of decision alternatives it is not possible to increase their pay-off in one value dimension without decreasing their pay-off in at least one other value dimension. In this sense the alternative chosen by the maximin rule dominates all the other alternatives.

The *procedural model* of responsible decision-making can be summarized as follows:
- (I) Framing the decision by
    - (i) identifying the applying ethical norms;
    - (ii) mapping out the affected parties;
    - (iii) defining goals and generating alternatives.
- (II) Multiple evaluations of the decision alternatives regarding
    - (i) the ethical norms;
    - (ii) the goals to be achieved;
    - (iii) the affected parties.
- (III) Finding the least worst alternative in the multidimensional space of deontological, goal-achievement, and stakeholder values.

There is always a conflict or at least some tension among the ethical norms, the decision maker's goals, and the interests of the stakeholders. Making a responsible choice is not an easy business at all. What is important is not the elimination of the conflict but to provide some *congruence* among ethical norms, the achievable goals, and the interests of the stakeholders.

4. Ethical and Social Justification of Profit Making

In business ethics the problem of justification of profit making is formulated in terms of social and ethical performance of business. In empirical studies that try to assess the social and/or ethical performance of business organizations deontological (norm-regarding) and stakeholder (other-regarding) aspects are often mixed up in a rather confusing way. Some conceptual clarification might be helpful.

I propose to define the *ethical performance* of a business organization as seeing its activities from the perspectives of the applying ethical norms. I propose to define the *social performance* of a business organization as seeing its impacts on the stakeholders.

Considering these definitions *evaluation procedures* can be developed to assess the ethical and social performance of business.

Let B be a *business organization* whose *activities* are $A_1,\ldots,A_i,\ldots,A_m$ during a *period* of *time* T. ($m \geq 1$) Let $D_1,\ldots,D_k,\ldots,D_p$ be *ethical norms* that are relevant in judging the activities of the business organization during the period of time under consideration. ($p \geq 1$)

An *ethical value function* $D_k(A_i)$ can be defined as follows:

$$D_k(A_i) = \begin{cases} 1 & \text{if activity } A_i \text{ } corresponds \text{ to ethical norm } D_k \\ 0 & \text{if activity } A_i \text{ is } neutral \text{ regarding ethical norm } D_k \\ -2 & \text{if activity } A_i \text{ } violates \text{ ethical norm } D_k \end{cases} \quad (12)$$

$D_k(A_i)$ characteristically shows the value of activity A_i regarding ethical norm D_k.

The following matrix reflects the ethical performance of business organization B during the time period T:

$$D(A) = \begin{array}{l} D_1(A_1),\ldots,D_1(A_i),\ldots,D_1(A_m) \\ D_k(A_1),\ldots,D_k(A_i),\ldots,D_k(A_m) \\ D_p(A_1),\ldots,D_p(A_i),\ldots,D_p(A_m) \end{array} \quad (13)$$

To get an overall picture of the ethical performance of business organization B during time period T we should introduce weights both for the activities and the ethical norms.

Let $x_1,...,x_i,...,x_m$ be *weights* that reflect the relative importance of activities $A_1,...,A_i,...,A_m$. Let $w_1,...,w_k,...,w_p$ be *weights* that reflect the relative importance of ethical norms $D_1,...,D_k,...,D_p$.

It is required that

$$\Sigma x_i = 1 \quad \text{and} \quad \Sigma w_k = 1 \tag{14}$$

The ethical performance of business organization B during time period T can be calculated as follows:

$$D(A) = \Sigma\Sigma w_k x_i \, D_k(A_i) \tag{15}$$

D(A) can be considered as a measure of ethical performance of business organization B during time period T. $(1 \geq D(A) \geq -2)$

Let P be the profit or other relevant indicator of *financial performance* of business organization B during time period T.

P is *ethically acceptable* if and only if $D(A) > 0$. This means that business organization B produced its profit P during time period T by activities $A_1,...,A_i,...,A_m$ that – in aggregate – do *not violate* ethical norms $D_1,...,D_k,...,D_p$.

Now let us turn to the question of social performance of business.

Let be $S_1,...,S_q,...,S_r$ *stakeholders* that are affected by the activities $A_1,...,A_i,...,A_m$ of business organization B during the period of time T. $(r \geq 1)$

A *stakeholder value function* $S_q(A_i)$ can be defined as follows:

$$S_q(A_i) = \begin{array}{l} 1 \text{ if activity } A_i \text{ is } good \text{ for stakeholder } S_q \\ 0 \text{ if activity } A_i \text{ is } neutral \text{ for stakeholder } S_q \\ -2 \text{ if activity } A_i \text{ is } bad \text{ for stakeholder } S_q \end{array} \tag{16}$$

$S_q(A_i)$ characteristically shows the value of activity A_i regarding stakeholder S_q.

The following matrix reflects the social performance of business organization B during time period T.

$$S(A) = \begin{array}{l} S_1(A_1),...,S_1(A_i),...,S_1(A_m) \\ S_q(A_i),...,S_q(A_i),...,S_q(A_m) \\ S_r(A_1),...,S_r(A_i),...,S_r(A_m) \end{array} \tag{17}$$

To get an aggregate picture about the social performance of business organization B during the time period T we should address weights to the stakeholders.

Let $v_1,\ldots,v_q,\ldots,v_r$ be *weights* that reflect the relative importance of stakeholders $S_1,\ldots,S_q,\ldots,S_r$. We can use the same *weights* $x_1,\ldots,x_i,\ldots,x_m$ for the activities of the organization.

It is required that

$$\Sigma v_q = 1 \qquad (18)$$

The ethical performance of business organization B during time period T can be calculated as follows:

$$S(A) = \Sigma\Sigma v_q x_i S_q(A_i) \qquad (19)$$

$S(A)$ can be considered as a measure of the social performance of business organization B during time period T. $(1 \geq S(A) \geq -2)$

Profit P is *socially acceptable* if and only if $S(A) > 0$. This means that business organization B produced its profit during period of time T by activities $A_1,\ldots,A_i,\ldots,A_m$ that – in aggregate – do *not cause harm* to stakeholders $S_1,\ldots,S_q,\ldots,S_r$.

The idea advanced here resembles the basic teaching of *Jewish economic ethics:* "Obey the Law and do not cause harm to anybody." (Tamari, M. 1987) *Non-violence* in one form or another is common in all the world religions. It is also at the heart of *Hindu* and *Buddhist ethics*.

Non-violence – both in the form of norm-regarding and stakeholder-regarding versions – emerges as a *necessary condition* of ethical and social acceptability of profit making. If we want to sustain business activities for a long time we certainly need a *less violent, more caring form* of profit making.

References

Albach, H. 1980. "Vertrauen in der ökonomischen Theorie." *Zeitschrift für die gesamte Staatswissenschaft* Vol. 136, no. 1: 3.

Alchian, A. A. & H. Demsetz. 1977. "Production, Information Costs and Economic Organization." In *Economic Forces at Work*, edited by A. Alchian, 73–110. Indianapolis: Liberty Press.

Arendt, H. 1961. *Between Past and Future. Six Exercises in Political Thought.* London: Faber and Faber Ltd.

Arrow, K. J. 1967. "Public and Private Values." In *Human Values and Economic Policy*, edited by S. Hook. New York: New York University Press.

Arrow, K. J. 1971. "Political and Economic Evaluation of Social Effects and Externalities." In *Frontiers of Quantitative Economics*, edited by M. D. Intriligator. Amsterdam: North Holland.

Arrow, K. J. 1972. "Gifts and Echanges." *Philosophy and Public Affairs*.

Auspitz, L., W. W. Gasparski, M. K. Mlicki, K. Szaniawski (eds.). 1992. *Praxiologies and the Philosophy of Economics*. New Brunswick & London: Transaction Publishers.

Banfield, E. C. 1958. *The Moral Basis of a Backward Society*. Glencoe, Ill: The Free Press.

Bateson, G. 1979. *Mind and Nature: A Necessary Unity*. New York: Dutton.

Baumol, W. J. 1975. "Business Responsibility and Economic Behaviour." In *Altruism, Morality and Economic Theory*, edited by E. S. Phelps. New York: Sage Foundation.

Becattini, G. 1999. "Possibilità e limiti dell'economia di mercato." *Economia e Politica Industriale*: 101–102.

Benjamin, M. 1992. "Compromise." In *Encyclopedia of Ethics*, edited by Lawrence Becker & Charlotte B. Becker, 189–191. New York & London: Garland Publishing, Ic.

Bocheński, J. M. 1992. *Contemporary methods of thinking*. Poznań: W drodze Publ. (in Polish)

Bocheński, J. M. 1993. "Zur Philosophie der industriellen Unternehmung." In *Logic and Philosophy*, Polish edition. Warsaw: PWN.

Bohata, M. 1996. "Some ethical Aspects of Transition and the Revival of Entrepreneurship in the Czech Republic." In *Human Action in Business: Praxiological and Ethical Dimensions*, edited by W. W. Gasparski & L. V. Ryan, 299–310. New Brunswick & London: Transaction Publishers.

Botturi, F. 1998. *Fenomenologia dialettica della libertè / Dialectic phenomenology of freedom*. Milan: mimeo.

Boulding, K. E. 1967. "The Basis of Value Judgements in Economics." In *Human Values and Economic Policy*, edited by S. Hook, 55–72. New York: New York University Press.

Boulding, K. E. 1969. "Economics as a Moral Science." *American Economic Review* 59.

Bowie, M. 1996. "The Moral Foundations of Capitalism." In *Human Action in Business: Praxiological and Ethical Dimensions*, edited by W. W. Gasparski & L. V. Ryan, 365–382. New Brunswick & London: Transaction Publishers.

Brennan, G. and Buchanan, J. 1981. "The Normative Purpose of Economic 'Science'." *International Review of Law and Economics*.

Bruni L. (ed.). 2000. *Economia di comunione*. Rome: Città Nuova.

Bruni, L. and Sugden, R. 1999. *Moral canals. Trust and social capital in the work of Hume, Smith and Genovesi*. Norwich (UK): mimeo.

Buchanan, J. M. 1954. "Social Choice, Democracy, and Free Markets." *Journal of Political Economy* no. 62: 114–123.

Buchanan, J. M. 1954. "Individual Choice in Voting and the Market." *Journal of Political Economy* no. 62: 334–343.

Buchanan, J. M. 1964. "What Should Economists Do?" *Southern Economic Journal* no. 30: 213–222.

Buchanan, J. M. 1965. "Ethical Rules, Expected Values, and Large Numbers." *Ethics* no. 76: 1–13.

Buchanan, J. M. 1969. "Is Economics the Science of Choice?" In *Roads to Freedom: Essays in Honour of Friedrich A. Von Hayek*, edited by E. Streissler. New York: A. M. Kelly.

Buchanan, J. M. 1978. "Markets, States, and the Extent of Morals." *American Economic Review* no. 68: 364–368.

Buchanan, J. M. & Tullock, G. 1974. *The Calculus of Consent*. 5th ed. Ann Arbor: University of Michigan Press.

Bunge, M. 1988. *Treatise on Basic Philosophy*, Vol. 8 *Ethics*. Dordrecht: Reidel.

Chakraborty, K. 1996. "Human Values and Indian Ethos." In *Human Action in Business: Praxiological and Ethical Dimensions*, edited by W. W. Gasparski & L. V. Ryan, 171–196. New Brunswick & London: Transaction Publishers.

Churchman, C. W. 1961. *Prediction and Optimal Decision, Philosophical Issues of a Science of Values.* Englewood Cliffs, N.J.: Prentice-Hall.

Dawes, R. M., van de Kragt, A. J. C. & Orbell, J. M. 1990. "Cooperation for the Benefit of Us – Not Me, or My Conscience." In *Beyond Self-Interest,* edited by J. J. Mansbridge, 97–110. Chicago & London: The University of Chicago Press.

Dembinski, P. H. 1995. "Financiarisation du Monde: les risques du non-sens." Instituto Jacques Maritain, International Conference *Economia, per quale futuro?* Rome, Nov. 30–Dec. 2.

Doi, T. 1973. *The Anatomy of Dependence.* Tokyo, New York, London: Kodanska. Japanese Original: *Amae no Kozo.* Tokyo: Kobundo, 1971.

Drucker, P. 1993. *Post-capitalist Society.* Oxford: Butterworth-Heinemann.

Dumont, L. 1977. *From Mandeville to Marx: The Genesis and Triumph of Economic Ideology.* Chicago: University of Chicago Press.

Dupuy, J. P. 1978. "L'economie de la morale, ou la morale de l'economie." *Revue d'Economie Politique* no. 88: 404–439.

Dylus, *Economy, Morality, Christianity.* Warsaw: Kontrast Publ. (in Polish)

Eggertsson, Th. 1992. *Economic Behaviour and Institutions.* Cambridge: Cambridge University Press.

Einaudi, L. 1942. "Preface to *Introduction to economic policy*" by C. Bresciani Turroni. Turin: Einaudi.

Elster, J. 1989. *The Cement of Society.* Cambridge: Cambridge University Press.

Etzioni, A. 1988. *The Moral Dimension.* New York: The Free Press.

Etzioni, A. 1991. "Eastern Europe: The Wealth of Lessons". *Challenge* (July–August).

Frankena, W. K. 1980. *Thinking About Morality.* Ann Arbor: University of Michigan Press.

Freeman, R. E. & R. A. Phillips. 1996. "Efficiency, Effectiveness, and Ethics." In *Human Action in Business: Praxiological and Ethical Dimensions,* edited by W. W. Gasparski & L.V. Ryan, 65–81. New Brunswick & London: Transaction Publishers.

Fritz, K. v. 1954. *The Theory of the Mixed Constitution in Antiquity.* New York: Columbia University Press.

Gasparski, W. W. 1987–1988. "On the concept of practicality." *Prakseologia* No. 101: 57–69 (in Polish).

Gasparski, W. W. 1995. "Praxiological Dimensions of Constructive Realism." In *Wissenschaft und Alltag,* edited by F. G. Wallner & J. Schimmer, 67–77. Wien: Wilhelm Braumüller Universitäts-Verlagsbuchhandlung G.m.b.H.

Gasparski, W. W. 1996. "Efficacious morality and ethical efficacy and the question of the economy resourcefulness." In *Ethical Dimension of Economic Transformation in Poland,* edited by A. Węgrzecki. Cracow: Cracovia Publ. (in Polish)

Gasparski, W. W. & L. V. Ryan (eds.). 1998. *Human Action in Business: Praxiological and Ethical Dimensions*. New Brunswick & London: Transaction Publishers.

Gasparski, W. W. 1998. "The Relevance of The Tadeusz Kotarbiński's Independent Ethics for a Participative Ethics in Business." *11th EBEN Annual Conference*. Leuven.

Gellermann, F. & Ladenson. 1990. *Values and Ethics in Organization and Human Systems Development: Responding to Dilemmas in Professional Life*. San Francisco: Jossey-Bass Publishers.

Gershuny, J. 1983. "Technical Change and Social Limits." In *Dilemmas of Liberal Democracies*, edited by A. Ellis & K. Kumar. London: Tavistock.

Gershuny, J. 1987. "Technical Change and the Work-Leisure Balance." In *Technology and Economic Progress*, edited by A. Sliberston. London: Macmillan.

Gilligan, C. 1982. *In a Different Voice*. Cambridge: Harvard University Press.

Goodpaster, K. E. & Matthews, J. B. 1982. "Can a Corporation Have Conscience?" *Harvard Business Review* no 1: 132–141.

Goodpaster, K. E. 1983. "The Concept of Corporate Responsibility." *Journal of Business Ethics* no 1: 1–22.

Goodpaster, K. E. 1996. "Praxiology and the Moral Agenda of Professional Education." In *Human Action in Business: Praxiological and Ethical Dimensions*, edited by W. W. Gasparski & L. V. Ryan, 437–453. New Brunswick & London: Transaction Publishers.

Grabher B. 1994. *The Elegance of Incoherence. Institutional Legacies, Privatization and Regional Development in East Germany and Hungary*. Berlin: Wissenschaftszentrum für Sozialforschung, Disc. Paper FS I94–103.

Grabher, B. 1994. "The Dis-Embedded Regional Economy. The Transformation of East German Industrial Complexes into Western Enclosures." In *Globalization and Changing Economic Prospects: Examples from Europe*, edited by Ash Amin and Nigel Thrift, 239–260. Oxford: Oxford University Press.

Grant, G. 1985. *English-Speaking Justice*. Toronto: House of Anansi Press.

Grosfeld, I. 1994. "Triggering Evolution: the Case for a Breakthrough in Privatization." Paris: *Delta*. Spring (mimeo).

Griffin, W. 1996. *Management*, 1993. 4th Edition. Houghton Mifflin Company (quoted after the Polish translation. Warsaw: Polish Scientific Publishers).

Hayek, F. A. von. 1968. *Der Wettbewerb als Entdeckungsverfahren*, Kiel: Institut für Weltwirtschaft.

Hayek, F. A. von. 1977. *Drei Vorlesungen über Demokratie, Gerechtigkeit und Sozialismus*, Walter Eucken Institut (Hrsg.), Vorträge und Aufsätze 63, Tübingen (J.C.B. Mohr [Paul Siebeck]).

Hayek, F. A. von. 1979. *The Counter-Revolution of Science*. 2nd ed. Indianapolis: Liberty Press.

Hayek, F. A. von. 1982. *Law, Legislation and Liberty*. London: Routledge and Kegan Paul.

Heap, Sh. H. 1989. *Rationality in Economics*. Oxford: Basil Blackwell.

Hegel, G. W. F. 1942. *Philosophy of Right*, translated with notes by T. M. Knox. Oxford. German Original: *Grundlinien der Philosophie des Rechts* (1821), Frankfurt a. M.: Suhrkamp, 1970.

Hiż, H. 1992. "Praxiology, Society and Ethics." In *Praxiologies and the Philosophy of Economics,* edited by J. L. Auspitz, W. W. Gasparski, M. K. Mlicki, K. Szaniawski, 421–429. New Brunswick & London: Transaction Publishers.

Hirsch, F. 1976. *Social Limits to Growth*. Cambridge, Mass.: Harvard University Press.

Hirschman, A. O. 1970. *Exit, Voice, and Loyalty: Responses to Decline in Firms, Organizations, and States*. Cambridge, Mass.: Harvard University Press.

Hirshleifer, J. 1978. "Competition, Cooperation, and Conflict in Economics and Biology." *American Economic Review* no. 68: 238ff.

Hutchenson, T. W. 1979. "Notes on the Effects of Economic Ideas on Policy: The Example of the German Social Market Economy." *Zeitschrift für die gesamte Staatswissenschaft* nr 135: 433 ff.

Inman, R. 1987. "Markets, governments and the new political economy." In *Handbook of Public Economics*, edited by A. Auerbach and M. Feldstein. Amsterdam: North Holland.

Jasinski, P. & Yarrow, G. 1995. *Privatisation: An Overview of the Issues*. Regulatory Policy Institute, Studies in Regulation, No. 4, Hertford College, Oxford.

Jencks, Ch. 1990. "Varieties of Altruism." In *Beyond Self-Interest*, edited by Jane J. Mansbridge, 53–67. Chicago & London: The University of Chicago Press.

John Paul II. 1996. "Addresses to Managers, Business People, and General Audiences." In *Human Action in Business: Praxiological and Ethical Dimensions*, edited by W. W. Gasparski & L. V. Ryan, 119–154. New Brunswick & London: Transaction Publishers.

Jonas, H. 1979. *Das Prinzip Verantwortung*. Franfurt am Main: Insel Verlag.

Jonas, H. 1984. *The Imperative of Responsibility*. Chicago and London: Chicago University Press.

Jonas, H.: *From Ancient Faith to Technological Man,* Bologna, Il Mulino, 1991. (in Italian)

Jones. 1982. *Business, Religion, and Ethics: Inquiry and Encounter*. Cambridge, Mass.: Oelgeschlager, Gunn & Hain Publishers, Inc.

Jünger, E. 1952. *Der Waldgang*. Frankfurt: Klostermann.

Kant, I. 1898. *Critique of Practical Reason*. London: Longmans, Green & Co. German Original: *Kritik der praktischen Vernunft* (1788), 1902 ff. Berlin: Akademie-Ausgabe der Preußischen Akademie der Wissenschaften, reprint 1968. Berlin: de Gruyter.

Kennedy, G. (ed.). 1994. *The Dignity of Work: John Paul II Speaks to Managers and Workers.* Canham, N.Y.: University Press of America.

Knight, F. H.: *The Ethics of Competition and Other Essays* (1935). Reprint Freeport, N.Y. (Books for Libraries Press) 1969.

Knight, F. H. 1947. *Freedom and Reform.* New York: Harper.

Kolm, S. 1994. "The Theory of Reciprocity and the Choice of Economic Systems." *Investigaciones economicas*: 67–95.

Kotarbiński, T. 1995. *Praxiology*, 2nd ed. Hull: Center for Systems Studies Press.

Kotarbiński, T. 1987. *Ethical Writings.* Wrocław: Ossolineum. (in Polish)

Koslowski, P. 1982. *Gesellschaft und Staat. Ein unvermeidlicher Dualismus.* Stuttgart: Klett-Cotta.

Koslowski, P. 1983. "Mechanische und organistische Analogien in der Wirtschaftswissenschaft – eine verfehlte Alternative." *Kyklos. Internationale Zeitschrift für Sozialwissenschaften* nr 36: 308–312.

Koslowski, P. 1987. "Market and Democracy as Discourses. Limits to Discoursive Social Co-ordination." In *Individual Liberty and Democratic Decision-Making. The Ethics, Economics, and Politics of Democracy*, edited by P. Koslowski, 58–92. Tübingen: J.C.B. Mohr [P. Siebeck].

Koslowski, P. 1989. *Wirtschaft als Kultur. Wirtschaftsethik und Wirtschaftskultur in der Postmoderne.* Wien: Edition Passagen.

Koslowski, P. 1991. *Gesellschaftliche Koordination. Eine ontologische und kulturwissenschaftliche Theorie der Marktwirtschaft.* Tübingen: J.C.B. Mohr [Paul Siebeck]).

Koslowski, P. 1995. "The Ethics of Banking. On the Ethical Economy of the Credit and Capital Market, of Speculation and Insider Trading in the German Experience." In *The Ethical Dimension of Financial Institutions and Markets*, edited by A. Argandona, 180–232. Berlin, Heidelberg, New York, Tokyo: Springer (= Studies in Economic Ethics and Philosophy, Vol. 8).

Koslowski, P. 1996. "Ecology and Ethics in the Economy." In *Ethical Universals in International Business*, edited by F. N. Brady. Berlin, Heidelberg, New York, Tokyo: Springer (= Studies in Economic Ethics and Philosophy, Vol. 9).

Koslowski, P. (ed.). 1997. *Business Ethics in East Central Europe.* Berlin––Heidelberg: Springer-Verlag.

Krings, H. 1980. *System und Freiheit. Gesammelte Aufsätze*, Freiburg: Alber.

Levi, I. 1986. *Hard Choices.* Cambridge: Cambridge University Press.

Loukola. 1996. "Background Institutions and Free Markets." In *Human Action in Business: Praxiological and Ethical Dimensions*, edited by W. W. Gasparski & L. V. Ryan, 283–297. New Brunswick & London: Transaction Publishers.

Luhmann, N. 1977. *Zweckbegriff und Systemrationalität. Über die Funktion Von Zwecken in sozialen Systemen.* 2nd ed. Frankfurt: Suhrkamp.

Macrae, N. 1981. "Für eine Welt individueller Lebensstile." In *Fortschritt ohne Maß? Eine Ortsbestimmung der wissenschaftlich-technischen Zivilisation*, edited by R. Löw, P. Koslowski, & P. Kreuzer, 213–233. München: Piper.

Mansbridge, J. J. 1990. "On the Relation of Altruism and Self-Interest." In *Beyond Self-Interest*, edited by Jane Mansbridge, 133–143. Chicago & London: The University of Chicago Press.

Margalit, A. 1996. *The Decent society*. Cambridge (Mass.): Harvard University Press.

Marshak, J. 1974. "Economic Planning and the Cost of Thinking." In *Economic Information, Decision and Prediction*, edited by J. Marshak, Vol. 2: 193–199. Dordrecht: Reidel.

Marx, K. 1977. *Manifest der kommunistischen Partei* (1848). In *Marx / Engels Werke*, Vol. 4. Berlin: Dietz.

Matel, A. 1996. "Ethical Leadership in a Free Society." In *Human Action in Business: Praxiological and Ethical Dimensions* edited by W. W. Gasparski & L. V. Ryan, 245–266. New Brunswick & London: Transaction Publishers.

Mathias, A. 1992. "Ethical Decision Making in India." In *Praxiologies and the Philosophy of Economics*, edited by J. L. Auspitz, W. W. Gasparski, M. K. Mlicki, K. Szaniawski, 311–327. New Brunswick & London: Transaction Publishers.

McCann, P. 1996. "Catholic Morality and the Knowledge Society." In *Human Action in Business: Praxiological and Ethical Dimensions*, edited by W. W. Gasparski & L. V. Ryan, 213–227. New Brunswick & London: Transaction Publishers.

McCann, P., F. B. Nasher & T. F. Duffy. 1996. "Implementing Praxiological Principles in Business." In *Human Action in Business: Praxiological and Ethical Dimensions*, edited by W. W. Gasparski & L. V. Ryan, 347–363. New Brunswick & London: Transaction Publishers.

McCloskey, D. 1992. "If you're so smart why ain't you rich?" In *Praxiologies and the Philosophy of Economics*, edited by: J. L. Auspitz, W. W. Gasparski, M. K. Mlicki, K. Szaniawski, 93–111. New Brunswick & London: Transaction Publishers.

Mertlík, P. 1995. "Czech Privatization: From Public Ownership to Public Ownership in Five Years?" *Prague Economic Papers* No. 4: 321–336.

Mises, L. von. 1968. *Human Action: A Treatise on Economics*. 3rd rev. ed. Chicago: Contemporary Books, Inc.

Mlčoch, L. 1992. "Czechoslovak Economy between the Past and the Future." *Prague Economic Papers* No. 2: 209–220.

Mlčoch, L. 1992. "Synthesis of Descriptive Analyses of a Traditional Model." *Prague Economic Papers* No. 4: 3ll–332.

Mlčoch, L. 1992. "Institutions in the Course of the Economic Transformation of Postsocialist Czechoslovakia." *Acta Universitatis Carolinae, Œconomica* (Prague) No. 1: 18–28.

Mlčoch, L. 1994. "The ethical Dimension of the Reestablishment of Private Property in the Czech Republic." In *Cultural Consequences of Economic Transition*. Troyes: Éditions Fates.

Mlčoch, L. 1995. "Privatization seen as the problem of institutional evolutionism." *Finance a úvěr* No. 4. (in Czech)

Mlčoch, L. 1995. "The Restructuring of Property Rights through the Institutional Economist's Eyes." *Prague Economic Papers* No. 2.

Mlčoch, L. 1997. "Czech Privatization – Penalties for the Speed. A Criticism of Radical Liberalism." In *Business Ethics in East Central Europe*, edited by P. Koslowski, 3–19. Berlin–Heidelberg: Springer-Verlag.

Mlčoch, L. 1998. "Czech Privatization: A Misunderstood Liberalism." *Journal of Business Ethics* July: 951–959.

Mlčoch, L. 1998. "Czech Style Capitalism." *New Presence* (Prague) July

Molina, L. de. 1602. *De justitia et jure*, Moguntiae.

More, S. 1990. *The Gita: A Theory of Human Action*. Delhi: Sri Satguru Publ.

Nagel, Th. 1970. *The Possibility of Altruism*. Princeton: Princeton University Press.

Nell-Breuning, O. v. 1955. "Neoliberalismus und Katholische Soziallehre." In *Der Christ und die soziale Marktwirtschaft*, edited by P. M. Boarmann. Stuttgart: Kohlhammer.

Nell-Breuning, O. v. 1974. *Kapitalismus-kritisch betrachtet*. Freiburg: Herder.

Nellis, J. 1994. "Is privatization necessary?" *FPD Note* No.7, World Bank, Washington, D.C., May.

Neumann, J. von & Morgenstern, O. 1944. *Theory of Games and Economic Behaviour*. Princeton: Princeton University Press.

Norman, E. R. 1979. "Denigration of Capitalism." In *The Denignation Capitalism: Six Points of View*, edited by M. Novack, 7–23. Washington, D.C.: American Enterprise Institute.

Nozick, R. 1974. *Anarchy, State, and Utopia*. Oxford: Basil Blackwell.

Ossowska, M. 1970. *Moral norms*. Warsaw: PWN. (in Polish)

Oxford Review of Economic Policy: "The assessment: the twentieth century – achievements, failures, lessons." *Oxford Review of Economic Policy*, 1999, Winter.

Pagano, U. 1990. *The Economics of Positional Goods*. Cambridge: University of Cambridge (mimeo)

Pelikán, P. 1993. "Privatization after Socialism: Why, when, and how." *Industrial Institute for Economic and Social Research*, Stockholm, October.

Pesqueux, Y. & B. Vergniol. 1996. "Firms, Business Ethics, and Society: From an Academic to a Protestant Standpoint." In *Human Action in Business: Praxiological and Ethical Dimensions*, edited by W. W. Gasparski & L. V. Ryan, 155–169. New Brunswick & London: Transaction Publishers.

Porta, P. L. & Scazzieri, R. 1997. *Towards an Economic Theory of International Civil Society*. University of Milan, Working Papers No. 3.

Posner, R. A. 1977. *Economic Analysis of Law*. Boston: Little, Brown.

Pszczołowski 1991. "Multiaspect Characteristics of Practical Realism." In *Logic, Practice, and Ethics: Messages of the Tadeusz Kotarbiński's Philosophy*, edited by W. W. Gasparski & A. Strzałecki. Warsaw: The Learned Society of Praxiology (in Polish).

Putman, R. 1993. *Making Democracy Work: Civic Traditions in Modern Italy*. Princeton: Princeton University Press.

Rowley, C.K. & Peacock, A.T. 1975. *Welfare Economics: A Liberal Restatement*. London: Martin Robertson.

Röpke, W. 1949. *Civitas Humana: Grundfragen der Gesellschafts-und Wirtschaftsreform*. Erlenback–Zürich: Rentsch.

Roscher, W. 1874. *Geschichte der Nationalökonomik in Deutschland*. München: Oldenbourg.

Ryan, L. V. "Management Education for the 'Triple E'." In *Human Action in Business: Praxiological and Ethical Dimensions*, edited by W. W. Gasparski & L. V. Ryan, 491–511. New Brunswick & London: Transaction Publishers.

Sacco, P. & Zamagni, S. 1998. *Civil Economy, Cultural Evolution and Participatory Development: A Theoretical Inquiry*. University of Bologna (mimo).

Salamon, L. 1999. "The nonprofit sector at a crossroads: the case of America." *Voluntas* No. 1.

Sauermann, H. (ed.). 1978. *Bargaining Behaviour*. Tübingen: J.C.B. Mohr [Paul Siebeck].

Schall, J. V. 1979. "Religion and the Demise of Capitalism." In *The Denigration of Capitalism: Six Points of View*, edited by M. Novack, 32–38. Washington, D.C.: American Enterprise Institute.

Scheler, M. 1966. *Der Formalismus in der Ethik und die materiale Wertethik*. 5th ed. Bern: Francke.

Schelling, F. W. J. 1975. *Philosophische Untersuchungen über das Wesen der menschlichen Freiheit* (1809), ed. W. Schulz. Frankfurt.

Schlicht, E. 1998. *On custom in the economy*. Oxford: Clarendon Press.

Schlosser, J. G. 1972. *Über das neue französische System der Policeyfreyheit, insbesondere in der Aufhebung der Zünfte* (About the new French system of police freedom, especially in the abolition of the guilds), *Kleinere Schriften* 1. Theil Basel 1787, Reprint New York/London (Johnso).

Scitovsky, T. 1976. *The Joyless Economy*. London: Oxford University Press.

Sen, A. 1967. "Isolation, Assurance and the Social Rate of Discount." *Quarterly Journal of Economics* No. 81: 112–124.

Sen, A. 1977. "Rational Fools: A Critique of the Behavioural Foundations of Economic Theory." *Philosophy and Public Affairs*: 317–344.

Sen, A. 1988. "Rights and Agency." In *Consequentialism and its Critics*, edited by Samuel Scheffler, 187–223. Oxford: Oxford University Press.

Sen, A. 1983. "Evaluator Relativity and Consequentialist Evaluation." *Philosophy and Public Affairs*: 113–132.

Sen, A. 1985. "Rights as Goals (Austin Lecture 1984)." In *Equality and Discrimination: Essays in Freedom and Justice,* editeds by S. Guest & A. Milne, 11–25. Stuttgart: Franz Steiner.

Sen, A. 1987. *On Ethics and Economics.* Blackwell.

Sen, A. 1993. "Markets and freedoms: achievements and limitations of the market mechanism in promoting individual freedoms." *Oxford Economic Papers* No. 45: 519–541.

Shackle, G. L. S. 1972. *Epistemics and Economics: A Critique of Economic Doctrines.* Cambridge: Cambridge University Press.

Shleifer, A. 1994. "Establishing Property Rights." *Annual Conference on Development Economics* April, The World Bank. Washington D.C.

Simon, H. A. 1978. "Rationality as Process and as Product of Thought." *American Economic Review* No. 2: 1–16.

Sombart, W. 1937. *Die Zukunft des Kapitalismus.* Berlin: Buchholz & Weißwange.

Soros, G. 1997. "The Capitalist Threat." *The Atlantic Monthly,* February.

Soros, G. 1998. *The Crisis of Global Capitalism.* London: Little, Brown and Company.

Spaemann, R. 1980. "Christentum und Kernkraft. Ethische Aspekte der Energiepolitik." *Die politische Meinung* nr 192 (Osnabrück).

Spencer, H. 1884. *The Man Versus the State.* Indianapolis: Liberty Classics. First ed. 1884.

Stahl, F. J. 1963. *Die Philosophie des Rechts.* 5 Vols., 1878, reprint Darmstadt.

Stark, D. 1996. "Recombinant Property in East European Capitalism." *American Journal of Sociology* No. 4: 993–1027.

Stegmüller, W. 1973. *Probleme und Resultate der Wissenschaftstheorie und Analytischen Philosophie. Personelle und statistische Wahrscheinlichkeit. 1. Halbbd.: Personelle Wahrscheinlichkeit und rationale Entscheidung.* Berlin: Springer.

Sternberg. 1994. *Just Business: Business Ethics in Action.* London: Little, Brown and Co.

Sternberg 1996. "A Teleological Approach to Business Ethics." In *Human Action in Business: Praxiological and Ethical Dimensions,* editeds by W. W. Gasparski & L. V. Ryan, 51–64. New Brunswick & London: Transaction Publishers.

Szelényi, I. 1995. "The Rise of Managerialism: The 'New Class' after the Fall of Communism." *Collegium Budapest, Discussion Paper* No. 16, Budapest, October

Tamari, M. 1996. "Determining the Criteria of Ethical Behaviour." In *Human Action in Business: Praxiological and Ethical Dimensions,* edited by W. W. Gasparski & L. V. Ryan, 197–211. New Brunswick & London: Transaction Publishers.

Trompenaars, F. 1993. *Riding the Waves of Cultures: Understanding Cultural Diversity in Business.* London: The Economist Books.

Uhlaner, C. J. 1989. "Relational Goods and Participation: Incorporating Sociability into a Theory of Rational Action." *Public Choice*: 253–285.

Weber, M. 1968. *Economy and Society*, edited by Gunther Roth & Claus Wittich. New York: Bedminster Press.

Weisskopf, W. A. 1971. *Alienation and Economics.* New York: Dutton.

Williamson, O. E. 1977. Firms and Markets. In *Modern Economic Thought*, edited by S. Weintraub. Philadelphia: University of Pennsylvania Press.

Williamson, O. E. 1981. "The Modern Corporation: Origins, Evolution, Attributes." *Journal of Economic Literature* No. 19: 1537–1570.

Wolfe, A. 1989. *Whose keeper? Social science and moral obligation.* Berkeley: University of California Press.

Wojtyła, K. 1979. *The acting person.* Dordrecht–London.

Zamagni, S. (ed.). 1995. *Economics of Altruism.* Allen Edgar.

Zamagni, S. 1997. "Economia civile come forza di civilizzazione della società italiana / Civil economy as civilizing force of Italian society." In *La società civile in Italia*, edited by P. Donati. Milan: Mondadori.

Zamagni, S. (1999a). "Valori e mercato." *Economia e Politica Industriale*, 101–102.

Zamagni, S. (1999b). "Social paradoxes of growth and civil economy." In *Economic Theory and Social Justice*, edited by G. Gandolfo and F. Marzano. London: Macmillan.

Zamagni, S. (1999c). "The significance of labour in a post-industrial society: unemployment and the role of civil economy," mimeo.

Zamagni, S. 2000. "Economic reductionism as a hindrance to the analysis of structural change." *Structural Change and Economic Dynamics* No. 3.

Zsolnai, L. 1997. "Moral Responsibility and Economic Choice." *International Journal of Social Economics* No. 4.

About the Contributors

Andrew Brody was born in 1924 in Budapest, Hungary. He has B.A. in mathematics from the Lorand Eötvös University and M.A. in Industrial Economics from the Karl Marx University of Economics, Budapest. He got his Ph.D. in Economics and D.Sc. in Economics from the Hungarian Academy of Sciences.

Since 1956 he has been working at the Institute of Economics of the Hungarian Academy of Sciences. Since 1977 he has been Scientific Adviser of the Institute. During his life-long affiliation with the Hungarian Academy of Sciences he was invited to work at various universities and research institutes.

From 1958 to 1964 Andrew Brody was lecturer in the Budapest Technical University. He was a Ford Foundation Scholar at Harvard University in 1964–1965. In 1970–1972 and 1974–1976 he was Professor of Economics and Head of the Department of Economics at Lusaka University in Zambia. In 1980–1981 he was Visiting Scientist in the Battelle Laboratories in the USA. He was Visiting Professor at Delhi University in India (1982), at Nice University in France (1987), at LaTrobe University in Australia (1991) and at Hitotsubashi University in Japan (1997).

Professor Brody's main field of research is input-output modeling and Von Neumann-Leontief type economic systems. His books include the following:

> *Slowdown: Global Economic Maladies*. 1985. Sage. London & New Delhi.
>
> *I.O. Techniques.* 1972. North-Holland. Amsterdam. (With A. Carter)
>
> *Proportions Prices, and Planning.* 1970. North-Holland. Amsterdam.
>
> *Contributions to I.O. Analysis.* 1970. North-Holland. Amsterdam. (With A. Carter)
>
> *Applications of I.O. Analysis.* 1970. North-Holland. Amsterdam. (With A. Carter)

R. Edward Freeman was born in 1954. He got a B.A. in Mathematics and Philosophy from Duke University. He received his Ph.D. in Philosophy from Washington University.

Professor Freeman joined the Darden Graduate School of Business of the University of Virginia in 1987 as Elis and Singe Olsson Professor of Business Administration and Director of the Olsson Center for Applied Ethics. Prior to going to the Darden School Freeman taught at University of Minnesota and the Wharton School, University of Pennsylvania.

Freeman's areas of interest are business ethics, strategy and leadership, and organizational studies. His books include the following:

Strategic Management: A Stakeholder Approach. 1984. Pitman.

Corporate Strategy and the Search for Ethics. (with D. Gilbert) 1987. Prentice Hall.

Business Ethics: The State of the Art. (editor) 1992. Oxford University Press.

Ethics and Agency Theory. (editor with N. Bowie). 1994. Oxford University Press.

Dictionary of Business Ethics. (editor with P. Werhane) 1997. Blackwell.

Professor Freeman is on the editorial boards of Business Ethics Quarterly and Research in Corporate Social Performance and Policy. He is the Editor of the Ruffin Series in Business Ethics published by Oxford University Press.

Freeman's current research projects are

Shades of Green: Business Ethics and the Environment (with J. Pearce and R. Dodd), an attempt to show how environmental values can be used to craft sustainable competitive advantage;

Managing for Stakeholders: Towards an Understanding of Capitalism, which seeks to give a modern account of capitalism for the next century.

Professor Freeman is a respected teacher. He has received the 6th Annual Outstanding Teaching Award from the Wharton Advisory Board, a Top Ten teachers Award from the Wharton MBA Program, and in 1986 was named Teacher of the Year at the Carlson School of Management at the University of Minnesota. In 1991 he was selected by the Class of 1991 to be a Faculty Marshall at Darden Business School. in 1993 he was chosen for the Outstanding Faculty Award by the Darden Student Body.

Wojciech W. Gasparski was born in 1936 in Warsaw, Poland. He got M.Sc. in Engineering form the Silesian University of Technology and Ph. D. from the Polish Academy of Sciences. He earned the title "Professor of Humanities" in 1985 in Poland.

Since 1967 he has been working at the Institute of Philosophy and Sociology of the Polish Academy of Sciences. Currently he serves as Chairman of the

Academic Board of the Institute and Head of the Research Group for Ethics in Economics and Business.

Professor Gasparski teaches at the American Studies Center of the Warsaw University, the Warsaw University of Technology, and the Warsaw School of Management. In addition, he is Consulting Faculty member at the Saybrook Institute in San Francisco. He was Visiting Scholar at the University of Helsinki, the State University of New York, and the Open University in England, the City University of London, and the Academy of Sciences in Moscow. He is Editor-in-Chief of the American series *Praxiology: The International Annual of Practical Philosophy and Methodology*. Also, he edits the Polish journal *Prakseologia*.

Professor Gasparski's books includes:

> *Action Learning*. 1998. Transaction, New Brunswick, N. J. (Edited with D. Botham)
>
> *Human Action in Business: Praxiological and Ethical Dimensions*. 1996. Transaction, New Brunswick, N. J. (Edited with L. V. Ryan)
>
> *Social Agency: Dilemmas and Education*. 1996. Transaction, New Brunswick, N. J. (Edited with B. H. Banathy)
>
> *Design & Systems: General Applications of Methodology*. 1995. Transaction, New Brunswick, N. J. (Edited with A. Collen)
>
> *Science in Society*. 1995. IFiS Publishers. (Edited with T. Airaksien)
>
> *A Philosophy of Practicality: Treatise on the Philosophy of Tadeusz Kotarbiński*. 1993. Societas Philosophica Fennica, Helsinki.
>
> *Understanding Design: The Praxiological-Systemic Perspective*. 1984. Intersystems, Seaside, CA.

Olivier Giscard d'Estaing was born on 30 December 1927. He got his Law Degree from the University of Paris and his MBA from Harvard Business School.

In 1958 Giscard d'Estaing founded INSEAD in Fontainebleau which became one of the top business schools in Europe. He served as advisor of big corporations including Phillips and IBM in France.

Giscard d'Estaing has been Chairman of BUSCO (Business Association for the World Social Summit) and the International Business Advisory Council of UNIDO. Also, he has been co-founder of Caux Round Table, which is dedicated to the ethical dialogue of multinational companies from USA, Europe and Asia.

Giscard d'Estaing published five book in French that are as follows:

> *Decentralisation des pouvoirs dans l'entreprise* (1963)
>
> *Education et Civilisation* (1968)
>
> *Le Social-Capitalism* (1976)
>
> *Maiastra, Renaissance de l'Occident* (1978)
>
> *L'homme du Salvador* (1988)

Peter Koslowski was born in 1952 in Göttingen, Germany. He earned his M.A. and Dr. Phil. in Philosophy and M.A. in Economics from the University of

Munich. From 1979 to 1985 he was Assistant Professor at the same university. From 1985 to 1987 he served as Professor at the University of Witten/Herdecke.

Since 1987 he has been Founding Director of the Forschungs Institute für Philosphie in Hannover. In 1996 he founded the Centrum für Ethische Ökonomie und Wirtschaftskultur in his Institute. He is also Adjunct Professor of Philosophy and Political Economy at the University of Witten/Herdecke.

In 1993 he was Visiting Professor at Jesus College in Oxford. In 1994 he was lecturing at Hitotsubashi University and other Japanese universities on the invitation of the Japanese Society for Promotion of Science. From 1991 to 1996 he was member of the Jury for Max Weber Prize for Economic Ethics. Since 1995 he has been directing the East–West Philosophy Project that aims the scientific exchange with Russia. Since 1997 he has served as Chair of the Committee for Economic Ethics of the Allgemeine Gesellschaft für Philosophie in Deutschland.

His books include the following:

> *Politik und Ökonomie bei Aristoteles.* 1976. Tübingen, Mohr Siebeck.
> *Ethik des Kapitalismus.* 1982. Tübingen, Mohr Siebeck. (With Chinese, English, Japanese, Korean, Russian, and Spanish translations)
> *Die Postmoderne Kultur.* 1987. München, C. H. Beck. (With Chinese, Italian, Japanese, Russian, and Ukrainian translations)
> *Prinzipien der Ethische Ökonomie.* 1988. Tübingen, Mohr Siebeck. (With forthcoming English, French, and Russian translations)
> *Die Ordung der Wirtschaft.* 1994. Tübingen, Mohr Siebeck.
> *Ethik der Banken und der Börse.* 1998. Tübingen, Mohr Siebeck.

Dr. Koslowski is the Editor of the Book Series *Ethical Economy. Studies in the Ethics, Culture, and Philosophy of the Economy.* The series is published in English by Springer-Verlag (Berlin & New York), in German by Physica Verlag (Heidelberg), in Russian by Institute Ekonomicseszkaja Skola (St. Petersburg), and in Chinese by China Social Sciences Publishing House (Beijing).

He also edits another book series *Philosophical Theology. Studies in Speculative Philosophy and Religion* published in German and English by Passagen Verlag in Vienna.

Lubomír Mlčoch was born on 13 May 1944 in Troubky, Czechoslovakia. After graduating in Economics he started to work at the Department of Political Economy, Prague School of Economics in 1967.

Between 1971 and 1988 he was on forced "sabbatical" for political reason. During this period Dr. Mlčoch served as economic researcher and planner at different socialist enterprises in the heavy industry and in the electric light industry. After 1988 he returned to the academic world.

In 1988–1990 he was researcher in the Institute of Economics at the Czechoslovak Academy of Sciences. In 1990–1992 he served as economic director of Concordia, the cooperative enterprise of the Czech catholic believers. In 1993–

–1996 he served as Head of the Department of Institutional Economics of the Charles University in Prague. Since 1996 Professor Mlčoch has been Dean of the Faculty of Social Sciences at the Charles University.

Mlčoch's publications include the first microeconomics textbook written in 1970 in the Communist Block. His book *The Behavior of the Czechoslovak Enterprise Sphere* was published in 1990 in Czech and in 1992 in English. His last book *Foggy Vision of Economic Transformation* (Karolinum, 1997) presents a critical diagnosis of mis-understood liberalism in the Czech Republic resulting in the erosion of order.

Ferenc Rabár was born in Budapest on 4 June 1929. He got his diploma from the State Business College in Budapest in 1949. From 1950 to 1960 he served as Accountant, Chief Accountant, Head of Planning Department and Head of Financial Department at various industrial and commercial firms. From 1960 to 1965 he served as one of the leaders of the Institute for Industrial Economics and Management.

In 1964 Mr. Rabar became Assistant Professor at the Technical University of Budapest where he taught mathematical programming. From 1965 to 1976 he was director of the INFELOR Systems Engineering Institute. In 1970 Mr. Rabár became Associate Professor at the Budapest University of Economic Sciences. From 1976 to 1980 he served as Program Leader at the International Institute for Applied Systems Analysis (IIASA) in Austria.

In 1990 Mr. Rabár became the Minister of Finance of the first freely elected Government of the Republic of Hungary. In 1991 he returned to the Budapest University of Economic Sciences where he received the "university professor" position. After his retirement he was appointed as Professor of Business Ethics at the Pázmány Péter Catholic University. He died on December 25 1999.

Professor Rabár's international scholarships include the following: Visiting Scholar at Nuffield College, Oxford (1965), Ford Scholar at Columbia University, Stanford University and Case Western Reserve University (1968–1969), and Visiting Scholar at New York University (1971).

Professor Rabár has published a lot of scholarly papers on simulation of large-scale economic systems, as well as on economic theory and economic policy.

Jörn Rüsen was born in 1938. He studied history, philosophy and German literature at the University of Cologne where he received his Ph.D. in 1966.

From 1969 to 1972 he taught philosophy at the University of Braunschweig. From 1972 to 1974 he taught at the Free University of Berlin. From 1974 to 1989 he was Professor of Modern History at the University of Bochum. Since 1989 he has been Professor of General History at the University of Bilefeld. Since 1997 he serves as President of the Institute of Cultural Sciences in Essen.

Professor Rüsen published 13 books and edited dozens of volumes in theory and methodology of history, historiography, modern intellectual history and historical consciousness.

George Soros was born in 1930 in Hungary. He survived the World War II living underground with his Jewish family in Nazi-controlled Budapest.

In 1947 Soros went to London where he enrolled at the London School of Economics. There he became under the spell of Karl Popper whose book *The Open Society and its Enemies* has profoundly shaped his later thought.

Soros pursued an extraordinary carrier in finance, first in London and then in New York. He spent much of his fortune during the 1980s fostering civic and human-rights activities in the communist Eastern and Central Europe. Since the collapse of communism his efforts have grown. In the late 1990 various foundations created by George Soros spent some USD 350 million.

Soros' most important publications include the following:

The Alchemy of Finance: Reading the Mind of the Market. 1987. John Wiley & Sons.

"The Capitalist Threat" *The Atlantic Monthly* 1997 February

The Crisis of Global Capitalism: Open Society Endangered. 1998. Little, Brown and Company.

Stefano Zamagni was born on 4 January 1943, in Rimini, Italy. He got his Masters Degree in Economics from the University of Milan. He received his Ph.D. from the University of Oxford under the supervision of John Hicks and Peter Hammond.

From 1973 to 1979 he was working at the University of Parma first as lecturer, later as chair professor of economics. In 1979 he became chair professor of economics at the University of Bologna where he has been teaching up till now.

From 1977 Professor Zamagni has been adjunct professor of economics at the Johns Hopkins University's Bologna Center. From 1985 he has been visiting professor at the University Bocconi in Milan. From 1994 he has been member of the Steering Committee of the Pontifical Academy of Social Sciences in Rome.

Professor Zamagni's books in English are as follows:

Microeconomic Theory. 1987. Oxford, Blackwell.

History of Economic Thought. 1993. Oxford University Press.

Value and Capital – Fifty Years Later. (with L. McKenzie) 1990. MacMillan, London.

Man-Environment and Development: Toward a Global Approach. 1991. Nova Spees, Rome.

Social and Ethical Aspects of Economics. (with I. Musu). 1992. Pontifical Council for Justice and Peace. Vatican City.

What Markets Can and Cannot Do: The Problem of Economic Transition in Central and Eastern European Countries. 1993. Nova Spes, Rome.

World Development and Economic Institutions. 1994. Pontifical Council for Justice and Peace. Vatican City.

The Economics of Altruism. 1995. Edward Elgar, Cheltenham.

Living in the Global Society. (with R. Papini and A. Pavan). 1997. Ashgate, London.

László Zsolnai was born on 5 May 1958, in Szentes, Hungary. He has Masters Degree in Finance and Doctoral Degree in Sociology from the Budapest University of Economic Sciences (BUES). He got his Ph.D. in Economics from the Hungarian Academy of Sciences.

From 1982 to 1987 he was Research Associate at the Department of Sociology of BUES. Since 1987 he has been working at the Department of Business Economics of the same University. Since 1995 he has been the Director of the Business Ethics Center of BUES. He is Chairman of the Business Ethics Inter--faculty Group of the Community of the European Management Schools (CEMS) in Paris. He is Tutor in Business Ethics at Warnborough University in London.

He was Director of the "Economics and Environmental Ethics," the "Ethics of Capitalism," and the "Business & Ecology" Summer Schools of the Central European University in 1997, 1998, and 2000. He was Convener of the first ever Transatlantic Business Ethics Summit in September 2000 in Budapest.

László Zsolnai is Editorial Board Member of the International Journal of Social Economics and Global Outlook: An International Journal of Business, Economics, and Social Policy.

László Zsolnai's most important publications include:

"Moral Responsibility and Economic Choice" *International Journal of Social Economics* 1997. No. 4.

The European Difference – Business Ethics in the Community of European Management Schools. 1998. Kluwer Academic Publishers, Boston–Dordrecht–London.

"Rational Choice and the Diversity of Choices" *Journal of Socio-Economics* 1998. No. 4.

Plurality of Values in Environmental Decision Making. OCEES Research Paper No 18. Mansfield College, University of Oxford. 2000 June

"Corporate Transgressions through Moral Disengagement" *Journal of Human Values* 2000 No. 1. pp. 57–64. (Co-authors: Albert Bandura & Gian-Vittorio Caprara)